外国语言学及应用语言学研究丛书

浙江师范大学外国语言文学省一流学科出版资助
2018年教育部人文社科一般项目阶段性成果（项目编号：18YJA740027）

A Corpus-Supported Approach to

Systemic Functional Grammar

语料库支撑的
系统功能语法研究

刘建鹏　著

ZHEJIANG UNIVERSITY PRESS
浙江大学出版社

图书在版编目 (CIP) 数据

语料库支撑的系统功能语法研究: 英文 / 刘建鹏著 .
— 杭州: 浙江大学出版社, 2020.5
ISBN 978-7-308-20141-4

Ⅰ. ①语⋯ Ⅱ. ①刘⋯ Ⅲ. ①语料库—功能（结构主
义语法）—研究—英文 Ⅳ. ① H04

中国版本图书馆CIP数据核字（2020）第059184号

语料库支撑的系统功能语法研究
刘建鹏 著

策　　划	张　琛　黄静芬
责任编辑	田　慧
责任校对	吴水燕　陆雅娟
封面设计	项梦怡
出版发行	浙江大学出版社
	（杭州市天目山路 148 号　邮政编码 310007）
	（网址:http://www.zjupress.com）
排　　版	杭州朝曦图文设计有限公司
印　　刷	广东虎彩云印刷有限公司绍兴分公司
开　　本	710mm×1000mm　1/16
印　　张	11.5
字　　数	253 千
版 印 次	2020 年 5 月第 1 版　2020 年 5 月第 1 次印刷
书　　号	ISBN 978-7-308-20141-4
定　　价	42.00 元

Contents

Chapter One
Introduction

The emergence and development of corpora and corpus linguistics (CL henceforth) have been changing and broadening the way of linguistic research. When commenting on the contributions of corpora to applied linguistics, Kawaguchi (2007: 32) suggests applying corpora to broader linguistic disciplines, "Linguistic corpora furnish a great variety of linguistic research domains and fruitful applications in language education, which I hope our readers will convince during their lectures of the present part. Thus, linguistic corpora have broadened our perspective of new research domains of linguistics and applied linguistics". Hunston (2002: 1) expresses a similar, but more penetrative idea by evaluating the influence of applying corpora to linguistic research, "it is no exaggeration to say that corpora, and the study of corpora, have revolutionized the study of language and of the applications of language over the last few decades". He emphasizes that corpora affect both linguistic research and application greatly.

The recent advancement in science and technology has proved and promoted the value of corpora and corpus linguistics to a large extent. Driven by modern information techniques, the capacity of corpora has been enlarged, and the functions of concordance software attached to corpora have been more delicate, concrete and powerful. As put forward by linguists like Hunston and Kawaguchi, the research with corpora of the real linguistic data has been increasingly introduced to more linguistic divisions. McEnery and Wilson (2001: 2) move on further and point out that corpora, as a methodology, can be used in almost all linguistic branch. Corpora have been widely used because they stresses the naturally-occurring real language and the research based on the statistics from the large-scaled linguistic data. Zong (2008: 10) confirms the value for the application of corpora to linguistic research: "Acquiring linguistic knowledge from a large amount of linguistic data is essential for the more objective and accurate penetration into the laws of natural language." As is said, corpora with the attached methodology are an indispensable approach to the true nature of language.

1.1 Background of the Study

Scholars of systemic functional grammar (SFG henceforth) have no reason for refusing corpora since the use of language in its social context has always been the foundation of the research on SFG. The social and natural use of language is the prerequisite for the linguistic research in both CL and SFG. Furthermore, the two have the same historical and philosophical basis, and regard language as a social phenomenon. In addition, both concentrate on the interrelationships between the choice of forms and the meaning realization under a socio-cultural context. As for the relationships between both branches, Wei (2007, 2009) concludes that both Halliday and Sinclair have adhered to the empiric ideas and methodology of their common tutor, Firth; besides, the application of the probabilistic profile to the linguistic research is recognized by both. It is the corpus that shortens the distance between meaning and form under contexts; it is the concordance that systematizes and regularizes the relationship between meaning and form. More importantly, corpora integrate linguistic form, meaning, function, psychology, society, culture, etc. into a whole that cannot be dismantled (Pu 2010: 44). Corpora should not be neglected because what is emphasized in SFG is that meaning is construed through the lexico-grammar of language.

Actually, corpora have been recognized and introduced to SFG for a long period of time, and Halliday (2004a: 34) points out that corpora are fundamental to the enterprise of theorizing language. One of the functions of corpora in theorizing language is to make it possible to represent grammar in quantity. What is more, the theme of the 29th International SFG Conference (held at the University of Liverpool) is "System and Corpus: Exploring Connections". How corpora and corpus linguistics are incorporated into SFG has been widely discussed in detail by scholars worldwide. Though different and even contrastive ideas were given on the relationship between corpora and SFG in the conference, the agreement reached finally by all was that there are synergies and complementarities between SFG and CL. The synergies and complementarities discussed in that conference can be concluded in three aspects: Thompson, Hunston, Stubbs, Hoey and Tucker stress a theoretical exploration into the problem of incorporating corpora and the attached methodology into SFG; in application, Matthiessen and Neale propose two contrastive approaches, that is, corpus-based and corpus-driven ones; Baldry, Thibault, and Sharoff try to find, in SFG, more extended areas explored by corpora and CL.

Halliday and Matthiessen (2004: 29) comment on the relationship between SFG and corpora: "A corpus is a large collection of instances of spoken and written texts; the corpora available now contain enough data to give significantly new insights into the grammar of English, provided the data can be processed and interpreted. But the corpus does not write the grammar for you...it has to be theorized." The comment can be concluded as follows: firstly, Halliday's constant shift of observational angle between two poles of system and text provides the space and possibility for a corpus approach to SFG; secondly, the subsidiary, supportive and data-persuasive value of the corpus approach is confirmed, so is the instrumental worth of the approach to penetrating into SFG and getting "significantly new" findings; thirdly, the corpus approach is preconditioned by the "processed and interpreted" data, namely, one aspect is that the data are expected to be annotated to make sense in corpus concordance, and the other is that conclusion is drawn by reading the retrieved lines and analyzing the statistical results; fourthly and most importantly, we should theorize on data, and theorization is an indispensable and necessary process in the way of finding new phenomena.

All the statements above can be different aspects of one problem, that is, the key to defining a corpus approach to SFG is to determine the position of the corpus approach in the space between system and instances. On the other hand, the emergence of huge corpora and the advanced technology make the instance end more plentiful and powerful, and SFG cannot ignore the new characteristics of the instances discovered by CL. A corpus way starts from large numbers of texts and reaches theory through instantiation, which is different from the traditional way of analyzing and/or theorizing on a single short text or several texts annotated manually.

With the development of modern science and technology of information, corpora and CL make the pole of instances huge in amount and clear in regularity, and the new orientation is expected to be noticed and studied to advance the development of the system pole in the linguistic research in SFG. Halliday does not ignore the changes in the pole of instances and proposes some guidelines and principles when applying the corpus to the research in SFG. Halliday's approach is corpus-based, and he emphasizes the annotated corpus data. Firstly, he suggests that the corpus be annotated or, at least tagged, because it is lexis-preferable. "It would be helpful to design a corpus so that some grammatical information could be built into the basic plan: for example (thinking of English), tagging of some of the more easily recognized markers..." (Halliday 2008: 73-74) The major way at present in SFG is corpus-based and a detailed systematic and comprehensive annotation of linguistic data is advocated by e. g. Matthiessen and Wu with their *SysFan*[1], O'Donnell with his *Systemic Coder*[2],

---

[1] *SysFan* is a computational tool developed by Christian Matthiessen and Canzhong Wu. The software facilitates the systemic-functional analysis of texts. *SysFan* is used to analyze the texts lexico-grammatically by making selections from menus, fields or networks, and save the records into a database, which can then be browsed, modified or searched. The search results can be statistically displayed or exported to those in a form compatible to statistical packages such as MS Word, or Excel (http: // minerva.ling.mq.edu.au/ Resources/ AnalysisTools/Tools.htm).

[2] *Systemic Coder* is a tool designed by Mick O'Donnell, and it facilitates the linguistic coding of texts. The user is prompted to categorise each text segment in terms of a system network, which the user provides. The statistical interface provides descriptive statistics on the codings, or statistical comparisons between subsets of the codings (http: // www. wagsoft. com /Coder/index.html).

Judd and O'Halloran with their *Systemics*[1], Bateman with his *Grammar Explorer*[2], etc.

However, the detailed theory-based manual annotation seriously confines the scale of the corpus, which is the precondition of the objectivity of a corpus-helped research. Furthermore, if some aspect of the theory in SFG is not sound, the conclusion based on the wrongly-annotated retrieval lines is, therefore, dangerous, unconvincing and even misleading. No tagged or annotated corpus applied by Sinclair is not what I mean to propose either because a corpus-driven approach wastes what we have achieved ever since. The corpus-driven approach is to find something free of the theoretical confinements and manipulations in SFG, and it is sporadic and superficial to induce purely from the retrieved lines in the corpus with fewer theories penetrating the data observation. Meanwhile, Halliday (2004a: 34) indicates that his corpus-based orientation is significant in linguistic research by saying that the corpus is fundamental to the enterprise of theorizing language.

Considered from the perspective of SFG, the research on the probabilistic nature of language deserves support and attestation by retrieving and observing a large amount of linguistic data. However, the present study on the corpus-based SFG is too theory-heavy to advance the development of the method because the corpus-related SFG research is short of a penetrative exploration and a comprehensive theoretical exploration and some concept confinements. What is more, the corpus-related SFG research, either domestic or abroad, ignores and even disobeys the disciplines and regularities of the concordance and annotation of linguistic data in the corpus at present, and all those rules guide the scientific and efficient process of linguistic data. The most foregrounding

---

[1] *Systemics* is designed by Kevin Judd and Kay O'Halloran. It is an efficient and comprehensive discourse analysis of texts from the perspective of systemic functional linguistics (SFL). *Systemics* is designed to be used for both academic and postgraduate research and also for the teaching of SFL in undergraduate and postgraduate courses (http://courses.nus.edu.sg/course/ellkoh/Overview.html).

[2] *Grammar Explorer* is a tool designed by John Bateman. It is developed for coding text examples, or for exploring KPML grammars. One can type in individual sentences, or specify a text file to load, with segment boundaries indicated. Results can be saved for later processing (http://www.fb10.uni-bremen.de /anglistik/ langpro/kpml/tools/grexplorer/grexplorer.htm).

obstacle in the incorporation of corpora and CL to SFG is that there is no definite and specific way to deal with the incompatibilities between CL and SFG. In addition, there is no guideline directing and regulating the research between the two subjects either. The situation results in various deviations and the research in that perspective has slowly come to an end. To be more specific, the misleading directions are: there is no research into the co-occurring probability of functions of the potential systemic members of a lexical class in construing meaning in figures; the annotation of linguistic data in corpora under a detailed framework of SFG is purely manual labor-intensive and time-consuming; there is no systemic idea or methodology in the application of corpora and corpus linguistics, etc. All the three above can be attributed to one reason: there is no proper approach to applying and incorporating corpus to the research in SFG. The approach is expected to be explored in a systemic and penetrative way.

The solution proposed in this study is a corpus-supported approach to SFG, different from either the corpus-based one (including grammar-based corpus and corpus-based grammar) advocated by Halliday and Matthiessen or the corpus-driven one by Sinclair. In this study, a proper and balanced way of how corpora are incorporated into SFG is expected to be explored from a novel perspective. The approach is expected to make the theoretical framework of SFG properly annotated in linguistic data in corpora; meanwhile, the annotation must be automatic or semi-automatic in order to make this way efficient and objective.

1.2 Purpose of the Study

The study aims to find a proper way of incorporating corpora and some theories of CL into SFG, and, ultimately, setting up a systemic and applicable approach with a theoretical basis. The approach is expected to start from the true character of the lexical preference of corpora and move on to find a proper approach to incorporating corpora and CL into SFG. The essence of the approach is to serve SFG in a corpus way in which all linguistic data concerned can be easily retrievable and annotatable; otherwise, corpora and CL will lose their worth in exploring and attesting the studies in SFG. The highly efficient automatic/semi-automatic concordance and annotation are essential, whose realization involves a reconsideration of the present corpus-based/driven SFG research. In addition, that is the prerequisite for the research into the probabilities of the meanings and functions of constituents and figures in construing meaning in the form of lexico-grammar. The application of corpora, theories and methodology of CL is available if the corpus way provides the possibility to make the formalized equation between the retrieved items in corpora and the functions in SFG. Therefore, the core of the approach to be explored is to model the theories in SFG into the retrievable and annotatable forms in CL. In general, the ultimate purpose of the book is to explore a corpus-supported approach to SFG that tries to realize an automatic/semi-automatic process of linguistic data based on a comprehensive elaboration of the synergies and complementarities between both the linguistic branches. The approach to be studied is different from both the corpus-based and corpus driven approaches that have ever been proposed before. It is expected to be a proper way to process linguistic data in a corpus way and make corpora and the attached methodology come closer to SFG in a more efficient way.

Specifically speaking, this book concentrates on the theoretical exploration and realization of a corpus-supported approach to SFG. The ultimate purpose of the book is to find new attesting and penetrating research ideas and means that are realized through the automatic / automatic process of linguistic data in corpora under the framework of SFG. The realization of the purpose depends on three different, but inter-related steps in succession: 1) to try to explore the inner relationship between SFG and CL, which is the prerequisite for and foundation of the proposition of a corpus-supported approach to SFG and determines the whole orientation of corpus-related SFG study; 2) to propose a corpus-supported approach to SFG, whose central ideas, experimental definition, major framework, content coverage and research means are sought for in accordance with the major principles and regularities of both SFG and CL; 3) to apply and realize a corpus-supported approach to SFG, that is to say, to fulfill some fuzzy semi-automatic syntactical annotations and the concordance of a linguistic feature under the theoretical framework of SFG. The annotation and concordance are key to the corpus-supported approach to SFG. The realization of both the annotation and retrieval resorts to the model, in which the theory of SFG is expected to be formalized, transformed or embodied in the specific strings, structure patterns and regexes that can be (semi-)automatically retrieved and annotated.

1.3 Significance of the Study

In both SFG and CL, it is advocated that linguistic research is to be based on the proof of real linguistic data, and forms, meanings, and functions are explained and described in accordance with the naturally-occurring linguistic data that are processed automatically and finally made into a probabilistic profile for a deeper research and discovery. Two deviations have arisen because we cannot properly incorporate corpora and CL into SFG. The first incorporation proposed by Matthiessen and Wu is corpus-based, which is too SFG-heavy because it annotates clauses in an exhaustive way under the theoretical framework of SFG. The way is too theory-heavy, labor-intensive and time-consuming to move on, and it has almost ceased going on since 2004. The other approach also goes to extreme, and its application of corpora is too theory-light. The approach uses corpora just as a potential source for choosing instances, and some intentionally-chosen instances are misrepresentative and, of course, hard to truly illustrate or describe a linguistic phenomenon. Both approaches are far from Halliday's ideas of theorizing language through corpora, namely, grammar-based corpora or corpus-based grammar.

However, Halliday himself does not give a comprehensive theoretical discussion and application of corpora and CL in the research of SFG. Almost all his papers relating to corpora tend to deal with the sporadic linguistic features in a limited corpus-based approach. The reason for the topic is that the corpus-based SFG has met the great challenges that have almost prevented the development of the approach. Specifically speaking, SFG has not been clear about in which way(s) they use corpora, corpus-based, corpus-driven or both. In the third edition of *An Introduction to Functional Grammar*, corpus application is very preliminary, a kind of informal use, in which Halliday and Matthiessen retrieve the corpus for examples that suit their purposes; besides, there is no systematic study of the mutual acceptance or inter-recognition in both theory and application; what is more, the annotation of corpora under the framework of SFG is still purely manual, which is the bottleneck of the growth of corpora. What is more, choosing instances from corpora is hard to be called corpus-based. Matthiessen has followed Halliday's annotated approach and established his *archives* that consists only of 6,500 clauses. All the data in *archives* are handily collected, that is, linguistic data are collected in a casual way, which are not Hallidayan. Halliday's corpus way is based on a large scale of corpora, "Large-scale quantitative studies of the relative frequencies of grammatical features, and their combinations, can reveal much about the underlying probabilistic patterns in the language... Corpus linguists have asked us to work towards 'corpus-based grammars'; in order to be able to do this we have to ask them, in turn, to work towards a grammar-based corpus" (Halliday 2008: 75). It is a problem that Matthiessen's grammar-based corpus is much too theory-heavy, which makes it small-scaled, less balanced and misrepresentative and thus less objective.

The solution to all the problems above is preconditioned by a systemic penetration into the relationships between SFG and CL in both theory and practice to find a more appropriate approach. The appropriate approach with the help of corpora reveals much more for SFG as follows:

1) making the research in SFG more objective and representative by reasoning on a large amount of linguistic data;

2) providing for a means of machine and software-supported approach to a large number of texts analyzed to supplement the present manual one;

3) making SFG attestable by checking the research in retrieved lines;

4) making the research in SFG more penetrative and piercing by showing the instance pole more clearly and deeply than any other means.

The specific solution is a corpus-supported approach, which is first proposed in the book. In that way, corpora and CL are properly incorporated into SFG, and the mutual synergies and complementarities between CL and SFG are explored. The real worth for the theoretical exploration and attestation through corpora is expected to be profitably employed by SFG in the corpus-supported approach. Only through corpora and CL can the probabilistic nature of language be actually realized, because a construction of the probabilistic profiles is based on the statistical numbers that must be acquired through retrieving and observing a large amount of linguistic data in corpora. The mode of the corpus-supported research will greatly refine and improve the research in SFG. The incorporation of corpora into SFG in that way makes the research in SFG more objective and comprehensive because all results are concluded from the proof of the attestable linguistic data through observing and reasoning on the real language use in a huge corpus. It is thus concluded that the proper incorporation of corpora and CL into SFG can make the research in SFG more objective and provide more persuasive and comprehensive proofs for linguistic description and attestation. In addition to the theoretical exploration, description and attestation, the corpus-supported approach can be an extended way for research. Meanwhile, the approach will advance the theoretical complementation and exploration in CL. Therefore, the corpus-supported approach is worth penetrating into systemically and comprehensively.

1.4 Layout of the Study

The study concentrates on the theoretical exploration and realization of a corpus-supported approach to SFG. The study aims to find a new attesting and penetrating research approach with the realization of a (semi-)automatic process of the linguistic data in corpora under the framework of SFG. Both the annotation and meaning concordance are key to the corpus-supported approach to SFG, and the realization of them resorts to a model, in which the theory of SFG is expected to be formalized or embodied in certain specific strings, structure patterns, and regexes (regular expressions) that can be (semi-) automatically retrieved and annotated. The modeling process consists of two aspects: modeling theories and theorizing on data. Modeling theories is the establishment of the theoretical models easy to come down to linguistic data and prone to being processed (semi-)automatically by concordance and coding software; theorizing on data is to observe linguistic data after coding and concordance, and reason on the observation and/or statistics of retrieved lines.

The study is arranged in three successive phases in general, and each of them is orientated to the common topic—a corpus-supported approach and its attached theory-modeling and theorizing on linguistic data. The three phases are given as follows: 1) to work out the theoretical basis and framework to prepare for and introduce the proposal of the concept of a corpus-supported approach; 2) to elaborate on the concept of the corpus-supported approach, from its definition, methodology, distinctive features and theoretical basis to its application; 3) to incorporate the corpus-supported approach to the ideational and textual metafunctions of SFG, and to try to work out the specific theoretical and applicable framework and model to make the approach more concrete and operable.

The first phase is dealt with in Chapter Two. The first part of Chapter Two deals with both SFG and CL to try to present the reasons for the introduction of a new way to get out of the stagnant situation at present. It gives the reason why it is necessary to give an introduction to the concept of a corpus-supported approach to SFG and then explains what improvements the approach can achieve. The second part of Chapter Two reviews the previous corpus-related SFG research and the resulting problems and contradictions. The corpus-based, corpus-driven, grammar-based corpus or corpus-based grammar cannot meet the challenges proposed by the practical research in SFG, because each of them is far from the real sense of the SFG research related to the corpus as Halliday expects.

The second phase is discussed in Chapters Three and Four. In the third chapter, the mutual synergies and complementarities between the theories of SFG and CL are further explored to figure out a new way that is expected to cope with the corpus-related SFG study systemically. Chapter Four is designed to work out the methodology, technology, modeling modes and the incorporation of corpora and CL into SFG in a corpus-supported approach to SFG. It is emphasized here that the core of the approach is to model modes, in which both CL and SFG are transformed into a certain form that can make both of them come closer. The modeling of modes consists of two parts: the first is to model the theories in SFG into a certain form easy to be retrieved and annotated by corpus technology; the second is to theorize on data retrieved in corpora under the framework concluded from both SFG and CL.

The third phase is dealt with in Chapters Five, Six and Seven. The tagging and annotation of linguistic data are separately dealt with in Chapters Six and Seven. The annotation of the ideational metafunction is coped with in Chapters Five and Six, and Chapter Seven concentrates on the textual metafunction. The reason for the separate dealing of the two metafunctions is that the two metafunctions have different ways of modeling theories. The novel idea reflected in the new corpus-supported approach to SFG is that the annotation of the syntactical information is made from the perspective of lexical preference instead of from the clause perspective. Chapter Seven is set separately because the textual metafunction is discussed in a distinguished way. In this chapter, two models are figured out in accordance with the distinctive characteristics of the lexical and grammatical cohesions. In the two general models, the micro-models are worked out to cope with the sub-classifications of the two cohesions.

Chapter Eight is the conclusions with the focus on what has been achieved in this book and what is for further research.

Chapter Two
Literature Review

Halliday advocates and practices a corpus-based approach to find out the probability profiles of language. To be specific, it should be the way in which numerous dependable proofs of linguistic data from corpora are employed to explain, check, attest, illustrate linguistic theories and describe linguistic phenomena. The concepts of the relative frequency, probability and corpora are, of course, applied as an important research method to reach the ultimate target of constructing the linguistic models in SFG. Before moving on to the major topic of this study, we'd better date back to Halliday's early works to find his original ideas on probability and corpora and learn the changes and development of the ideas in recent years. The retrospection is not only necessary but also enlightening.

2.1 Halliday's Works Related and Other Views on Corpora

2.1.1 Frequency, Probability and Quantitative Methods

As is discussed in Webster's (2005: vii) introduction to Halliday's collected works, namely, *Computational and Quantitative Studies*, Halliday proposes his ideas of applying the theory of frequency and probability of language to machine translation in his two articles: "The Linguistic Basis of a Mechanical Thesaurus, and Its Application to English Preposition Classification" and "Linguistics and Machine Translation". Both articles show that the mechanism of machine translation is to build the models of systemic relation of one linguistic description to another. Therefore, the description of language precedes the realization of equation in two languages.

It is concluded that the descriptive model of language is key to machine translation. Halliday has proposed his views on the descriptive model of language applied in machine translation. His model consists of two parts that are realized in three steps. The first part of the model is to find out the translation equivalence between the categories of two languages by ordering elements into systems within which determination operates in accordance with the criteria governing the choice among the elements ranged as terms in the system of the set language; the second part is to set up these categories into a thesaurus, whose series form a continuous string of lexical analogues of the grammatical paradigm (Halliday 1962). The realization of the equation mechanism with its two parts consists of three steps that are stated as follows:

> First, there is the selection of "the most probable translation equivalent" for each item at each rank, based on simple frequency. Second, there is the conditioning effect of the surrounding text in the source language on these probabilities: here grammatical and lexical features of the unit next above are taken into account and may (or may not) lead to the choice of an item other than the one with highest overall probability. Third, there is the internal structure of the target language, which may (or may not) lead to the choice of yet another item as a result of the grammatical and lexical relations particular to that language: these can be viewed as brought into operation similarly by step-by-step progression up the rank scale. (Halliday 1962: 31)

It can be figured out from Halliday's explanation that the core of the realization of Halliday's translation mechanism in machine translation is to find the most probable equivalents from the lexical thesaurus of both languages and arrange the thesaurus in a grammatical paradigm in both languages, which is the first phase of looking for translation equivalents. But, my question is, how does he find the most probable equivalents from the lexical thesaurus of both languages? Whether for the thesaurus equivalents or the grammatical ones (series of the thesaurus in the grammatical paradigm), what is of the first importance is to find the relative frequency of a word in the thesaurus or grammatical equivalents in order to set up the probability profiles of the use of all the lexical members of a thesaurus or a structure of thesaurus series. Establishing the grammatical equivalents is based on the probability profiles of the lexical thesaurus, in which the former is more complicated than the latter. Halliday (1962: 27) has statements as follows: "Grammatical equivalence between two languages can be displayed most adequately, therefore, by means of quantitative studies of the grammar of each. Such equivalence must furthermore be related to the rank scale: the scale of grammatical units, of which the word is one. These units are the stretches into which language text is cut when grammatical statements are being made about it." Therefore, a quantitative study of the relative frequency of lexical members in the thesaurus is the prerequisite for the further establishment of the grammatical probability profile in which the lexical one serves as a constituent.

What is discussed above indicates that only through a quantitative method can the ratio of relative frequency of the lexical and grammatical features and the probability profile be realized through retrieving and making statistics of a huge amount of linguistic data in a corpus way. The quantitative methodology of the corpus is explained and practiced in Halliday's two later articles: "Quantitative Studies and Probabilities in Grammar" (1993a) and "A Quantitative Study of Polarity and Primary Tense in the English Finite Clause" (1993b). In the first article, Halliday (1993a: 156) comments on the quantitative way as follows, "…and whether or not there is any significance in the particular quantitative study reported here, with the potential for quantitative research opened up by corpus linguistics our understanding of language…". His words indicate that he supports the quantitative way and confirms the revealing value of the method. In the second article, Halliday and James have practiced his quantitative research method and studied the frequency and distributions of primary tense in English finite clauses. In the work, the quantitative method is highly valued as "basic" by Halliday, "the aim of this study was to undertake some basic quantitative research in the grammar of Modern English" (Halliday 1993b: 93). The quantitative way of research into SFG describes and reveals the grammar or linguistic features of a more intuitive, concrete and perceivable approach to the abstract theory. Specifically speaking, quantitative methods in SFG demonstrate the (relative) frequency of linguistic features and its distributions through statistical profiles, and the results are easy to read because the foregrounding statistical numbers suggest something regular in a more direct way. In addition to an easy apprehension, the quantitative research can be more illuminating because the statistical profiles derived from the naturally-occurring objective linguistic data usually imply more than what a researcher has expected previously.

2.1.2 Probability and Corpora in SFG

In linguistics, the most basic statistical element is frequency, which is, in fact, a kind of probability that describes the number or possible number of times of the appearance of a linguistic feature. The concentration on the probability of language features in linguistic research has thus produced a new linguistic discipline, that is, probability linguistics. Commenting on probability and linguistic research, Aarts (1999) argues that the observation on frequency is a means instead of a purpose, and its purpose is to observe a question and answer a question and move from quantity to quality. In recent years, probability-based linguistic research has been greatly developed. Gui (2004: 4) concludes that probability linguistics, computational linguistics, corpus linguistics and psychological linguistics are all frequency and probability-based, and they show their obedience to the tradition of complying with facts of language. Linguistics returns to the facts of language for further well-founded research. Sampson (1987) puts forward three features of probabilistic means: 1) the probabilistic means depends on the application of the analytical techniques of the statistics of linguistic features instead of the absolute logical rules; 2) the focus is on the real linguistic data in indefinite texts instead of the instances invented or coined by some linguistics; 3) statistics of real and natural linguistic data are more powerful than those of pre-selected ones. Gui (2004: 8) points out, "probabilistic means is not only a method, but a kind of thought". The appearances of things (including the use of language) are a probabilistic phenomenon. The major strongpoint of probabilistic means is that it provides not only the positive proofs but also the negative ones. He confirms that probabilistic means is worth valuing and advocates the probability-based linguistic research. The precondition of probability-based linguistic research is to collect linguistic data and build corpora.

As is touched on in the section above, language is probabilistic in nature in SFG and the linguistic probability profile can be built up through a quantitative study of the relative frequency of the lexical and grammatical features. Meanwhile, we can say, in turn, that the probability profile concluded from the instance pole is the quantitative statistical profile of the system pole. So, the quantitative approach to describing and discovering the system in SFG starts from a statistical study of the linguistic features in instances. Therefore, a good question is how to make the instance pole representative in variety and large enough in amount in order to ensure that the final statistics are objective in building the final system profiles. In addition, the quantitative approach can be extended for the study of register varieties of language and other attesting research areas like testing a hypothesis.

If the idea of the probabilistic nature of language is vague and indefinite in the two articles cited above, Halliday (1991a: 45) confirms the view and elaborates on it in his paper "Towards Probabilistic Interpretations".

> Frequency in text is the instantiation of probability in the system. A linguistic system is inherently probabilistic in nature. I tried to express this in my early work on Chinese grammar, using observed frequencies in the corpus and estimating probabilities for terms in grammatical systems (1956, 1959). Obviously, to interpret language in probabilistic terms, the grammar (that is, the theory of grammar, the *grammatics*) has to be paradigmatic: it has to be able to represent language as **choice**, since probability is the probability of "choosing" (not in any conscious sense, of course) one thing rather than another.

Firth's concept of "system", in the "system/structure" framework, already modeled language as choice. Once you say "choose for polarity: positive or negative?", or "choose for tense: past or present or future?", then each of these options could have a probability value attached.

It can be deduced that the choice of the meaning potential system is the choice of probability when an instantiation happens and moves from the system pole to the instance pole, and it can thus be derived that language originates from the probabilistic choice, and grammar is the regular probabilistic profile of language choice. To be more specific, the grammar in SFG is the representation of the paradigmatic choice profiles in both the horizontal (colligation) and vertical (choice in system) perspectives. It can thus be inferred that, in SFG, system is computed and modeled in the quantitative study of instances. Actually, Halliday (1991a: 46) has done the similar things in his early research, "when I was constructing my original system networks for English in the early sixties, I counted some grammatical frequencies, noting the occurrences of different terms in some of the primary systems, to see if any general principles of frequency distribution suggested themselves" (see Halliday 1976). The approach from instance pole to the system pole has been confirmed and applied in Halliday's research. Besides setting up general theory, the approach is also applied to exploring the pre-existing theories like finding out the recursive and non-recursive systems, the diachronic research into the children's language development and the system variation in semantic choice in target text(s).

Concerning the probability and register variation, Halliday (1991a: 60) explains, "...it is the probabilistic profile of lexico-grammar that enables us to explain register variation. Register variation can be defined as the skewing of (some of) these overall probabilities, in the environment of some specific configuration of field, tenor and mode". Meanwhile, he adds, "...every text is in some register, just as every text is in some dialect—that is, every text is located somewhere in dialectal and diatypic space. This means that the greater the variety of texts examined, the more accurate the picture will be; it requires a lot of observations to approximate to a quantitative profile of the grammar of a language..." Halliday points out that the large number of texts from the varieties of registers is the assurance of the objectivity and comprehensiveness of the quantitative approach of research, but how can the requirement be realized? The corpus is the means only through which can the task be performed.

Halliday confirms the corpus and its relationship with probability in his article "Corpus Studies and Probabilistic Grammar" (1991b) and emphasizes the value of the corpus in SFG research by saying, "There is no longer any need to argue for the importance of corpus studies as a source of information about the grammar of a language, and indeed as a source of insight into the nature of grammar in general" (1991b: 63). Halliday (1991b: 67) then explains their relationship, "...a paradigmatic grammar, based on the concept of the 'system' in Firth's sense of the term, frequency information from the corpus can be used to establish the probability profile of any grammatical system. From this profile—the probabilities of each of the terms—we can derive a measure of the information that is generated by that system..." In the two comments above, Halliday makes the point that the corpus is the source and instrument with which system can be built into probability profiles and each element of grammar can find its meaning value in the statistical profiles. Therefore, the value of the corpus has been firmly set in the research of SFG.

In the article above, the register study based on the corpus is extended and probability is made clearer, "a corpus which is organized by register, as all the great first generation ones have been, makes it possible to study such external conditioning of probabilities, and to show how the grammar of doing science differs quantitatively from that of telling stories, advertising and so on" (Halliday 1991b: 71). Register study here based on the corpus can be moved from the specific features of texts to the more general register framework. That movement is preconditioned by the corpus that contains a large number of texts chosen with the consideration of representation and variety of genres. In addition to being applied to study registers, the corpus can be used in the diachronic language acquisition of a child (Halliday's son) by Hasan and linguistic features by Nesbitt and Plum (1988). It can be said that corpus studies have a central place in modeling probability of linguistic features and linguistic system.

The value and importance of the corpus are asserted in Halliday's other two articles: "Language as System and Language as Instance: The Corpus as a Theoretical Construct" (1992), and "The Spoken Language Corpus: A Foundation for Grammatical Theory" (2002a). In the first article, as Halliday (1992: 84) puts forward, "'a register' is a syndrome of lexico-grammatical probabilities". The "syndrome" here refers to the possible combinations of variants. The corpus is compared to the bi-directional medium through which system is built out of the instances that can be abstracted in the form of probability profiles close to system. The corpus serves as the instantiating instrument mediating between the system pole and the instance pole of the same continuous whole of lexico-grammar. In the midway of the instantiating process, a profile of register is turned out with the character of foregrounding certain linguistic features in the probabilistic profile. Furthermore, register is also a variation of system before reaching the instance pole. In the second article, Halliday (2002a: 177) says, "I have been trying to suggest, in this chapter, why I think that the spoken language corpus is a crucial resource for theoretical research: research not just into the spoken language, but into language in general". This shows Halliday's original approach to linguistic research starts from the corpus of instances and moves to grammatical system in SFG research, that is to say, theorization is based on the corpus observation. The way is explained in detail in his comment as follows: "But the principle behind corpus linguistics is that every instance carries equal weight. The instance is valued as a window onto the system: the potential that is being manifested in the text. What the corpus does is to enable us to see more closely, and more accurately, into that underlying system—into the langue, if you like." (Halliday 2002a: 174) The function of the corpus is highly valued in modeling instances into probability profiles to indicate or produce the system of certain aspects of language. Here the research into the spoken language based on the corpus is unidirectional, that is, the study starts from the corpus to theory. As is suggested in the title of the second article, the corpus is the foundation for theory in SFG.

2.1.3 Applications of Corpora to SFG

Actually, Halliday's research starts with the application of corpora, and he has noticed the importance of corpora and made great achievements with corpora a long time before. In his doctoral thesis, Halliday (1971) studies grammar from the perspective of both quantity and probability to try to find a way of applying quantitative methods to establishing the relational network between different grammatical systems. Halliday (1992: 77) emphasizes, "But the systems in question were clause systems, and one needed very large numbers of occurrences. If, as it appeared, there was typically a difference of about one order of magnitude (ten to one) in the relative frequency of unmarked and marked terms, such as positive/negative or declarative/interrogative, then to get anywhere beyond the least delicate grammatical categories we were going to need not thousands of clauses but hundreds of thousands for reliable numerical." Halliday proposes four key points for the corpus-based SFG research in his ideas above:

1) corpus-based SFG is at the clause level;

2) the corpus is huge;

3) comparison between the corresponding linguistic features is the method;

4) the units to be researched at the clausal level are to be studied as grammatical constituents of clause.

Both the first and the last points suggest that the corpus-based study of SFG deals with the meaning with reference to the usage in real linguistic data; the second and the third indicate that the proper scale of the corpus and method of research ensure the objectivity of this approach. Furthermore, Halliday stresses the importance of the corpus and confirms the necessity of the corpus in SFG study by stating "Corpus studies have a central place in theoretical investigations of language. There are many ways in which a corpus can be exploited, of which the one considered here—by no means the only one—is that of providing evidence of relative frequencies in the grammar, from which can be established the probability profiles of grammatical systems" (1991b: 73). Halliday here gives the definite purpose of SFG study on the corpus and the method of reaching the purpose. The purpose of applying corpora to the research of SFG is to build the probability profiles of the specific systems of grammar; the way to realize the purpose is to search the linguistic data to find the evidence and establish the frequency-based interrelationships of all system constituents by reasoning on observed evidence data and the statistical patterns or results. Later on, Halliday is more deeply engaged in his corpus-based SFG study, writing the article "A Quantitative Study of Polarity and Primary Tense in the English Finite Clause" (1993b), which is based on 18 million words of written texts chosen from COBUILD built by Sinclair and concluding the specific proportions of polarity and primary tense.

Fries (1957: 37) discusses Halliday and his SFG, corpora and corpus linguistics, "Halliday has long claimed that information concerning the relative frequencies of the various options within a system should be considered part of the system itself. Such a position entails that linguists have some basis for describing these frequencies. Hence SFL has made considerable use of corpora and corpus linguistics. Of course, the field of corpus linguistics is commonly regarded as a brand-new approach to linguistics which has developed and become popular over the past forty years—since the development of computers. Like all new fields, however, its roots lie in earlier forms of the discipline". Fries recognizes and supports Halliday's incorporation of corpora and ideas of CL into SFG through applying corpora and the means of CL to discovering the relative frequency of options of the lexical-grammatical units at all the levels in the functional system of language; meanwhile, he emphasizes the methodological and instrumental functions of CL in other linguistic schools and foresees that the development of the new information technology will boost other disciplines of linguistic research. The importance of corpora in SFG study, especially in counting and making statistics of the relative frequencies of the various options within a system, is the reason for our more attention and efforts to learn further about the relationship between the two subjects. Both corpora (including their attached software) and CL have changed a lot with the advancement of modern science and technology, and thus SFG is expected to catch the new changes and characteristics.

The relationship between SFG and corpora was further explored in detail in the 29th International Systemic Functional Congress (held in 2002), and the topic of the congress was "systemic and the corpus: exploring the connections". In the congress, Hunston (2006) and Hoey (2006) held a view that is in contrast with the approach Halliday has been undertaking. Both of them believe a corpus-driven approach comes closer to the nature and regularities of language than a corpus-based one held by Halliday.

To be more specific, they both believe that the introduction of corpus linguistics to SFG is to move from the observation of language instances to an explanation of those instances. They both hold the viewpoint that SFG can be a theoretical guidance for CL and a large number of real instances and their particular re-occurring patterns should be accounted for in social-cultural contexts guided by certain theory. In addition to that, Stubbs (2006: 15-35) also thinks that the combination of CL and SFG is more corpus-heavy, and he advocates a corpus-driven approach to the theoretical linguistic and cognitive models from the social perspective. Hoey's suspicion of SFG is more obvious than the three corpus-driven advocators above, and he says as follows, "Although systemic functional theory posits a more sophisticated and satisfying account of the relationship between grammar and lexis, there are still difficulties in squaring the notion of system as classically posed and the insights currently being derived from corpus linguistics" (Hoey 2006: 37). Hoey (2003, 2004, 2005, 2006) takes the corpus-driven approach and studies the priming prosody of lexical colligation, the semantic association and the grammatical and textual colligation. His reason for the corpus-driven way is that the choice in the potential meaning system is not just the choice of a lexical item or grammar, but also the choice of the lexical item and its collocations, colligations and semantic associations.

Hunston's phraseological approach (2006: 56-80) is also corpus-driven in nature and he insists on the phraseological study of the prospection pattern of lexico-grammar revealed through the corpus concordance and observation. He holds such a view because he thinks the probability is also to be reset for each lexical item and sequence in addition to that probabilities to be reset for each register (Halliday 1991b). Tucker (2006: 81-102) is greatly concerned with how

SFG responds and reacts to corpus findings. However, different from Halliday, Tucker (2006: 82) shows his similar worries, "Systemic functional linguistics is itself centrally concerned with the analysis of text. Why and how, therefore, does corpus-based linguistic research constitute a challenge that theories and descriptions need to address". Meanwhile, he (2006: 83) adds, "the large language corpus is the crystallized and condensed reflection of human linguistic experience. More importantly, it allows us to observe the patterns, regularities and irregularities of linguistic behavior which are directly inaccessible in the normal course of experience". In Tucker's views above, it is asserted that he prefers a corpus-driven approach in his research, and his focus is on the probabilistic syntagmatic patterns and tendencies ranging across the lexico-grammatical sequences and texts.

Neale is another corpus-driven approach follower, and she (2002) concentrates on modifying and extending the transitivity system in SFG with the linguistic data proofs retrieved from corpora. Specifically speaking, in her approach, she makes the second use of the collected data from the West and Collins COBUILD English Dictionary and sets up her own small corpus of 5,400 verb senses named PTDB, and she believes that her corpus-driven approach is bi-directional by developing a system network out of lexis and into grammar, and out of grammar into lexis. In addition, Sharoff's study on size adjectives (2006: 184-205) and Hori's research into the pain expressions in Japanese (2006: 206-225) are corpus-driven, too.

All the scholars above support a corpus-driven approach. Though their specific research methods are a little different, they all think SFG can be more delicate and objective by being set under corpora for attestation, modification and extension, all of which can only be achieved through corpus concordance and observation. Meanwhile, the corpus-based approach of Halliday has its supporters, one of whom is Matthiessen.

Matthiessen (2006: 103) contends for his corpus-based views at the beginning of his report, "Corpus-based methodology and text-based research have played a central role in Systemic Functional Linguistics since the beginning, in fact, since before this framework began to be called 'systemic functional'". One of his students, Wu (2006) has also done the similar related research. Wu (2000) and Matthiessen (2006) have designed several software tools of annotation and concordance under the framework of SFG and made a detailed probability profile of certain aspects of system. Wu, with the help of the software called *SysFan* designed by himself and Matthiessen, annotates less than a hundred sentences to establish the probabilistic profile of the themes of ranking clauses, thematic referents in the conversation, thematic referents in the conversation subject, finite and systemic features, systemic selections in the system network of mood system, selections of different speakers, relative frequencies of systemic selections, process types and ergative functions, systemic selections in the system of transitivity, distribution of process types in relation to agency, distribution of systemic features according to speakers, distribution of process types in relation to polarity, distribution of polarity within process types and distribution of process types within polarity.

Following the research from the perspective, Matthiessen penetrates into the study further and creates his *archives,* a small corpus containing 6,500 clauses, which is more large-scaled than Wu's. Matthiessen's (2006) research based on *archives* covers the relative frequencies of manner, intersection of taxis and logico-semantic type (relative frequencies), depth of nesting and variation in taxis and logico-semantic type, frequencies of instantiation in basic textual, interpersonal and experiential systems of the clause, intersection of agency and process types, intersection of process types and circumstantiation, instantiation of certain circumstantial selections across the different process types and interpersonal system of clause (mood type intersected with process type, mood type intersected with process type logarithmic scale, mood type intersected with polarity and indicative type and mood person), and his conclusion is that there is a well-established relationship between the frequency of instantiation and the extent along the syntagmatic or structural axis of organization. Matthiessen's study concentrates on correlations between the patterns of instantiation along the cline of instantiation and the patterns of systemic elaboration along the paradigmatic axis.

However, Matthiessen's real research is not based on corpora, but on *archives* which consists of 6,500 manually-annotated clauses collected by himself in a casual way. Matthiessen adheres to a pure manual annotation of clauses, and his purpose is to establish the probabilistic profile of the metafunctions and intersections of the simultaneous systems. The probabilistic profiles of instantiation are set up in a corpus-based way because annotation is made at the clause level under the framework of SFG at the very beginning of the research.

In addition to Matthiessen and Wu, Baldry and Thibault's research on the system of multimodal corpus linguistics (2006: 164-182) is also corpus-based because the data collection and analysis are much too theory-heavy; Miller's higher level of intertextual appraisal of "giving" in the small corpus of Alma Mater donation is SFG-assisted from beginning to end, and appraising the retrieved lines from the corpus is under the framework of SFG. Kaltenbacher's (2006: 269-292) research into the emotive expressions and the factual culture-related linguistic differences in tourist websites is completely corpus-based, because the encodings of the interpersonal function of the data in the corpus are under the appraisal system in SFG.

Halliday makes comments on both the corpus-driven and corpus-based approaches. Concerning the former, Halliday (2006: 297) proposes, "I think most of those who have worked in the systemic functional framework would agree with Gordon Tucker, that corpus studies and systemic theory come together naturally in the course of researching into lexical grammar. The modeling of patterns at this stratum, in particular those that fall towards the lexical end of the continuum, collations, fixed and semi-fixed expressions and the like, cannot now be seriously undertaken without reliance on the information derived from large-scale corpus investigations". The comment indicates that Halliday confirms the objective and revealing value of the corpus-driven approach based on a large-scaled corpus. Meanwhile, Halliday (2006: 299) puts forward his views on the corpus-based approach when referring to Matthiessen' report, saying "… Matthiessen's results, apart from now substantiating this from the data, add new dimension to the explanation of the power of language as semogenic system". It is obvious that Halliday supports the enterprise of a small-scaled corpus-based research and believes the value and the truth in the research supported by a small number of manually-annotated clauses. Halliday's views on the incorporation of corpora and CL into SFG in 2004[1] and 2008[2] have almost shown no changes, and they will be introduced in detail in the next chapter.

2.2 SFG and a Corpus Approach

A brief review of SFG is preferred for having a better understanding of a corpus approach to SFG.

2.2.1 SFG

2.2.1.1 *Linguistic Theory and Theoretical Modeling*

As for the status quo of American linguistic study, Zheng et al. once comment, "there is a problem in American linguistic study: too many linguistic theories, but short of linguistic materials, which is not sound" (Zhang et al. 2002: 77). Whether a linguistic theory comes from a linguistic observation or logic reasoning, it must go back to linguistic material to be checked to attest its value in describing linguistic phenomena. Therefore, the testing standard to judge one theory is reasonable or not is to see whether it properly describes a language or a large amount of linguistic data. It is thus proposed that theory is expected to be tested and linguistic data need to be introduced to make linguistic theory return to where it comes from to find its worth. Linguistic theory should not be something too high to be reached by the real linguistic data, and it needs the help of data to come down to the earth. However, abridging linguistic theory and data are not a direct and simple equation, and it is required that linguistic theories should be formalized into some expressions reachable by linguistic data. In return, the linguistic data study is expected to be concluded in the form of some string or certain combination in order to come close to linguistic theories. Before moving to the abridging process, we'd better learn more about either side.

---

① Refers to the third edition of *An Introduction to Systemic Functional Grammar.*
② Refers to *Complementarities in Language.*

The first prerequisite question to be answered clearly is what a linguistic theory actually is. Concerning the understanding of a linguistic theory, Nesbitt (1994: 243) thus comments, "Theory is a semiotic resource for making meaning in description: description is given value through theory. Since theory is a system of meanings, it gives a higher-level organization to the meanings made in description. The richer the theory we have at our disposal, the richer we can make our description". He claims above that the major value of theory consists in describing linguistic data. Richer theories are fuller description.

The theoretical framework of SFG is just the kind with a comparatively complete theoretical system including all strata about language, ranging from phonology, lexical grammar and semantics to context. In SFG, linguistic data are defined as instances with reference to the definition of a language that is regarded as a resource for making meaning. The meaning potential system with three stratifications consists of semantics, lexico-grammar and phonology, each of which is a potential resource concerning a specific order of abstraction. The transition and connection of all the three levels are related by realization from the highest level to the lowest one (Matthiessen 1995; Halliday & Matthiessen 1999). The lower level is generalized across various domains defined by a higher level (Halliday, 1973), and a higher one is generated from an abstraction from a lower one. For example, semantics is realized by lexico-grammar, which is again realized by phonology.

Generally speaking, SFG has a complete theory system that runs from phonology and semantics to context, including stratification, instantiation, metafunction, axis and rank, through all of which language models are construed for linguistic description. Meanwhile, SFG research areas are widely broadened and deeply explored in many perspectives and, to be specific, the theoretical system can be applied to construing the different descriptive models of a language for the various research areas. Different kinds of theoretical models are built in distinct disciplines, and a few examples are listed here: language education (e.g. Rothery 1989; Christie 1991), speech pathology (e.g. Armstrong 1991), text generation (e.g. Fawcett & Tucker 1990; Mann & Matthiessen 1983; Matthiessen et al. 1991, 1998; Bateman et al. 1991), and text analysis (e.g.

Kasper 1988; O'Donnell 1994).

2.2.1.2 Seminal Ideas in SFG

SFG originates from Firth, the founder of British linguistics and the creator of London School, who critically inherits some essentials from both Malinowski and Saussure. Here we trace back to him for more revealing linguistic ideas on the nature of language. In the two books (*Speech*, 1930; *The Tongue of Men*, 1937) and forty one papers by Firth, his basic viewpoints on language are clearly described. He accepts Saussure's ideas of structure and rejects the distinction between langue and parole, especially opposing the linguistic point that linguistics is the study of langue instead of parole. Rethinking on Saussure's linguistics, Firth develops "system" and "structure" and alleges that system is vertical and paradigmatic while structure, horizontal and paradigmatic in nature. The essence of Firth's linguistics contains two focuses: one is that the object of linguistics is the real language use; the other is that the ultimate purpose of linguistic research is to establish the equations between linguistic factors and non-linguistic ones. Here the non-linguistic factors refer to the experience created when we interact with the surrounding world (including the inner world), and the establishment of the equations between linguistic factors and non-linguistic ones is actually the same process of describing the human experience with language. Malinowski's influence on Firth is the consideration of the social culture situation and situational context. To be more concrete, Malinowski's ideas expand the limits of Firth's definition of meaning and create the meaning in both linguistic and non-linguistic context, in other words, the meaning comes out of, besides lexis and grammar, the linguistic environment involving society, culture, belief and the whole factors of participants.

Halliday inherits and develops Firth's theory and makes his system more concrete and comprehensive. Firth's sporadic ideas and theories are organically connected to make all levels of theories interrelated closely by Halliday. The foregrounding contribution by Halliday is the set-up of construing modes bridging the space between linguistic factors and non-linguistic ones, namely, the relationship between meaning represented by lexical-grammar and experience outside language.

Halliday's new ideas about language mainly consist in the context of situation and system. Here the context of situation is studied from the perspective of sociology besides the typical social situations by Firth, and the social semiotics in linguistics is proposed as an additional complementation. System is fully developed by creating a set of complete categorizations and defining their interrelationships. Specifically, in Hallidayan linguistics it is considered that language is a social semiotic potential system and has three metafunctions i.e. ideational, interpersonal and textual, four stratifications consisting of phonology, lexico-grammar, semantics, context, and two organizations including paradigmatic and syntagmatic axes.

It can be summarized that the systemic functional theory centers on the functions of constituents of figures in construing experience, enacting social relationship and organizing texts. Language is semantic and socially-semiotic, and SFG concentrates on texts instead of clauses. In SFG, all the theoretical models are the modes for construing language into a semiotic system of a higher-order which is the potential system describing language in general terms. Three strata are defined as follows (Halliday 1985; Matthiessen & Bateman 1991; Matthiessen 1995):

Semantics: the meaning represented by linguistic constituents (lexico-grammar) and the potential resource of meaning. It is the medium and interface, through which the non-linguistic system and the lexico-grammatical system are abridged. It is the semantic stratum that makes the inner or outside world known, namely, it is the description of our inner or outside experience. The result of a semantic construction is the text. Besides, the semantic environment relates the text to the non-linguistic social context, enabling us to act by means of meaning.

Lexico-grammar: the system of grammar and lexis and the potential resource (grammatical & lexical constituents) for construing meaning. Lexis (words) is the most delicate grammar; therefore, grammar and lexis are not distinct, but in a cline. Lexico-grammar is also the elastic space between meaning and experience.

Phonology: the resource for sounding, including intonation, rhythm, syllabic structure and phonological shape. For it is not closely related to the topic of this study, it is thus not worth elaborating in detail.

The explanation above treats lexico-grammar as an abstract medium between phonology and semantics, and it is distinctive from the other two strata since it has no direct interface with material phenomena. Semantics interfaces with human experience and social processes. Lexico-grammar is an elastic space between semantics and phonology, which makes language distinctive and creative in generating an infinite number of meanings.

The relationship between one stratum and its neighbors is that of realization: lexico-grammar realizes semantics; phonology realizes lexico-grammar. The connections between phonology and lexico-grammar are fixed, but the ones between grammar and semantics are uncertain though grammatical categories are the linguistic classifications of semantic categories (Matthiessen & Bateman 1991; Matthiessen 1995).

Instantiation is similar with realization at another level. Between the meaning system pole in potential and the instance pole in reality is instantiation, whose original result is the clauses in texts. Nesbitt (1994: 54) comments that instantiation is a dimension of a theory by which meaning potential is instantiated in texts as the instantialized potential. Here the instantialized potential refers to the linguistic realization (in the form of morpheme, word, phrase clause or text) of the meaning in the potential linguistic system. Each linguistic model has its unique and school-featured classification of both poles of system and text. Saussure's *langue* and *parole* and Chomsky's *competence* and *performance* both consider system and text as distinctive phenomena of language, in which *parole* and *performance* are the general conceptualizations, but not the specific linguistic realization of the instances. *Langue* and *competence* are language abstraction that is regarded as the language acquisition device instead of the system of language itself and the context (situational linguistic context and social-cultured context). On the other hand, the treatment of both poles of language in SFG is not a discreet dichotomy, but a cline continuum, or a cline of instantiation in which text and system are two different classified understandings of the same phenomenon. As for further apprehension, we can turn to Halliday's analogical illustration by using the relationship between *climate* and *weather* as a reference to demonstrate instantiation as follows (Halliday 1991c: 42):

> Climate is instantiated in the form of weather; today's temperature, humidity, direction and speed of wind, etc. in central Scotland are instances of climatic phenomena. As such they may be more, or less, typical: today's maximum is so many degrees higher, or lower, than average—meaning the average at this place, at this time of the year and this time of day. The average is a statement of probabilities: there is a 70% chance, let us say, that the temperature will fall within such and such a range. The probability is a feature of the system (the climate); but it is no more, and no less, than the pattern set up by the instances (the weather), and each instance, no matter how minutely, perturbs these probabilities and so change the system (or else keeps it as it is, which is just the limiting case of changing it). The climate and the weather are not two different phenomena. They are the same phenomenon seen by two different observers, standing at different distances—different time depths. To the climate observer, the weather looks like random unpredictable ripples; to the weather observer, the climate is a vague and unreal outline. So it is also with language: language as system, and language as instance. They are not two different phenomena; they are the same phenomena seen by different observers. The system is the pattern formed by the instances; and each instance represents an exchange with the environment—and incursion into the system in which every level of language is involved. The system is permeable because each instance redounds with the context of situation, and so perturbs the system in interaction with the environment.

The elaboration above states that instantiation is the process moving from the abstract and inclusive pole towards the concrete and specific one that can be seen and touched. And either end of instantiation has its unique characteristics that must be leant in detail respectively. What is more, the moving process and the result are the emphases that we should focus on because both of them can better explain the whole instantiation and both poles of language.

Register is closely related to instantiation, and it is the variation of instantiation according to contexts. Register refers to the regions covering texts and systems along the cline of instantiation, and it can thus be apprehended from two perspectives. From the instantiation one, register is seen as a cluster of similar texts or text types, while from the potential one, it is the variation in the system (a subsystem). Therefore, a specific register is a region of some span covering a phase in the cline of instantiation, and there is a kind of freedom to move around in some extension in the cline of instantiation. "We can investigate a text, and see how a particular linguistic system is instantiated in this particular text; we can also go beyond the single text, and look for the recurrent patterns in sets of texts in order to characterize text types or the overall linguistic system, which is a typical methodology in corpus linguistics, and a common approach to domain modeling in computational linguistics" (Wu 2000: 36).

As a linguistic research means, a comprehensive linguistic application of register to linguistic data analysis and theoretical promotion should cover both the specific instantiation and the potential system, and the interrelationships between them. Besides its importance in SFG, register is also a key concept in CL, which, in most cases, abides by the principle of register from the start to the end in its discipline research. Originally, most corpora are built by collecting the texts of the same register or many registers. In both the corpus-based and corpus-driven research, as for analyzing the retrieved linguistic data, only the data from the same register can be comparable in most cases. Finally, the last stage of theorizing on data depends on grasping the general features of linguistic data of the same or approximate register. In addition to all those brought up, the register with the cline running over the two poles is also especially imperative in the annotation in CL because tagging is realized at the instance end. In addition, the tagging rules come from and abide by the linguistic potential system.

2.2.1.3 Modes of the Realization of Metafunctions or Instantiating Modes

In SFG, language is a meaning potential, which is divided into three modes of meaning or three metafunctions according to the functions a language can realize: ideational (logical and experiential), interpersonal and textual metafunctions. These three metafunctions are simultaneous but functionally unique in the linguistic system, which can be summarized as follows:

Ideational metafunction: the potential resource for construing our experience of the inner or outside world. The ideational metafunction consists of two subdivisions: the experiential and the logical. In the former, experience is construed through figures, the constituents of which are process, participant and circumstance, while in the latter, the framework of experience is established as the network by means of two general abstract relations: interdependency and logical-semantic relation. Halliday (1985, 1994, 2004a) shows the views that any two different language units share an interdependency, which can be further divided into parataxis and hypotaxis, and the logical-semantic relation can be classified into expansion and projection in general. Of course, these can be sub-classified into various subdivisions for a more detailed description. In general, the experiential metafunction is realized by the transitivity structure and the logical metafunction by parataxis and hypotaxis.

Interpersonal metafunction: the potential resource for enacting social relationships between speakers and listeners. In the complete mood system, speakers are regarded as the intruders of the meaning potential, through which speakers are situated in certain situational context to express their attitudes and judgments and try to affect others. What is more, the mood system plays an important communicative role in exchanging commodity (goods & services, information) between the speaker and the listener. The communicative role and exchanging commodity are combined to form the four imperative functions: offer, command, statement and question.

Textual metafunction: the potential resource for construing texts by transforming the ideational and interpersonal realization into certain kind of information organization that is the interface through which a text is developed into its related context. The grammatical realization of that function is the thematic structure, information structure and cohesive devices.

All the three dimensions are of equal importance in the meaning instantiation and realization. In conclusion, the metafunctions are both lexico-grammatical and semantic. The whole linguistic structure in context is determined by strata, metafunctions and instantiation, while the inner structure of each stratal region is regulated by axis, rank and delicacy (Halliday, 1978, 1985; Halliday & Matthiessen, 1999). The meaning is construed through the three metafunctions and the instantiation of each of them. The hierarchy of stratification divides language into a number of strata, each of which is organized locally into a hierarchy of units or ranks. Each rank is organized internally along two axes of organization: the systemic or paradigmatic axis and the structural or syntagmatic axis. The systemic or paradigmatic axis is ordered in delicacy from the more delicate systems to the less delicate systems, and the systems are organized into a system of systems or a system network. The system network provides the paradigmatic context for a system, and the system is located with respect to all other systems within the system network (Matthiessen & Bateman 1991; Matthiessen 1995; Zeng 1996; Wu 2000).

Such an idea is indicated in the two sections above, corresponding to the ideational, interpersonal and textual metafunctions respectively. Variation of meaning at the contextual level can be equally divided into field, tenor and mode. The correspondence of metafunctions to the three variation sub-forms is, in essence, the same phenomenon viewed from the distinctive perspectives. If we say that the register discussed in the section above is the model through which text types are realized, the definitions and functions of metafunctions suggest that they be models through which three distinctive dimensions of meaning are established. Modeling metafunction is the one that shapes the abstract meaning into the concrete semantic or logico-semantic linguistic form or structure. The goal of a corpus-supported approach to SFG is to realize the formalization of the models to make them (semi-)automatically annotated and retrieved. The models have been formed from the observation and theorization on data, and they can thus be dated back to linguistic data, that is, the lexical-grammatical form to find the lexico-grammatical representation of the models, which ensures the possibility to formalize the metafunctional models into the proposed lexico-grammatical forms.

2.2.1.4 Lexico-grammar

Concerning the lexis and grammar, Halliday (1961: 267) has spoken of a grammarian's dream, "the grammarian's dream…is to turn the whole of linguistic form into grammar, hoping to show that lexis can be defined as 'most delicate grammar'". Hasan (1987:185) explores the possibility of establishing a lexico-grammatical network in delicacy for the purpose of describing and producing lexical items by bringing in the nine distinct lexical items: *gather, collect, accumulate; scatter, divide, distribute; strew, spill, spare*. Here lexical verbs are treated as part of the transitivity region of grammar, and the systems to generate the items are more delicate choices within the "material" Process. Wu (2000: 96-98) gives a good summary as follows: Fawcett and Tucker's (1990) thought of lexis as the most delicate grammar has been explored by a number of researchers since the issue was first raised as an implemented systemic model in the COMMUNAL project[①], in which systemic features are considered to be at the semantic level and motivated by both functional and formal criteria. Cross (1991) develops a model of lexis in HORACE[②] for text production in the register of the environmental texts primarily by using the ideational meaning of the lexical item. Nesbitt (1994) treats lexis and grammar as a single unified resource in the EDA (Electronic Discourse Analyser) project, which is intended to develop an NLP system that assists translators and editors in the production of grammatically correct English text appropriate for technical computer system documentation. Matthiessen makes a fairly extensive exploration into the ideational meaning of lexis at different ranks, but at the same time emphasizes that lexical choices potentially reflect all the three metafunctions, each of which makes a specific contribution to lexis. Matthiessen (1995: 110-111) proposes:

---

① COMMUNAL project is a computational linguistics unit presided by Robin Fawcett, Gordon Tucker and other scholars in Cardiff University. COMMUNAL is a piece of software and a sentence generation system developed in the project. It doesn't generate from semantic input, but rather requires the user to traverse the system network, choosing a feature at each point.

② HORACE is a piece of text-generation software developed by Cross.

...from an ideational point of view, that lexis is, concerned with denotation and it is organized as taxonomies of things, events, and so on; that is, it is a taxonomic interpretation and representation of our experience of the world. From an interpersonal point of view, lexis is concerned with connotation—with meanings concerned with the relationship between speaker and listener and the speaker's intrusion into the speech situation; these meanings include formality and politeness as well as affect. From a textual point of view, lexis is concerned with the creation of text—with continuity in text, textual boundaries, and so on.

The above discussion by Matthiessen clarifies the relationship between metafunctions and lexis. As has been touched on before, lexis is the most delicate part of grammar, and the span between lexis and grammar is a continuum of a unified linguistic system, namely, lexico-grammar. "The extension of lexis into grammar means that the systems in the lexical part of lexico-grammar are organized in the same principle as those in the grammatical part..." (Wu 2000: 98). Based on Halliday's (1961), Matthiessen's (1995) and Wu's (2000) viewpoints, it can be concluded that, on the one hand, the meaning of a word is determined by its delicate position in the system of lexico-grammar, to be more specific, in the three metafunctional representations; on the other hand, this determination is mutual, and the choice of lexis decides the grammar or metafunctions in return because the lexical selection suggests choosing certain micro-grammar or micro-metafunctions that guide the realization of a full grammar. What is more, the choice of lexis and its attached micro-grammar are the will-be basic pattern of metafunctions from the perspective of construing meaning. Furthermore, the penetration into the deciding relation shows that it is mutual and bi-directional: from the angle of text analysis, lexis is determined by its position in grammar; from the meaning-construing or text-generating perspective, lexis decides grammar.

2.2.1.5 Realization of Meaning Through Lexico-grammar

The discussion above shows that language is a potential resource for making meaning, in whose system, besides the relationship between metafunctions and lexico-grammar, the three strata, namely semantics, lexico-grammar and phonology, are also related by realization (Halliday 1985, 1996, 2004; Halliday & Matthiessen 1999). A lower stratum is a generalization across the various domains defined by a higher stratum (Halliday 1973: Ch. 4), and a higher stratum constitutes an abstraction over a lower stratum. More specifically, semantics is realized by lexico-grammar, which is again realized by phonology. Similarly, meta-language is "a resource for construing our experience of language" (Halliday & Matthiessen 1999: 30), and can also be stratified into different levels of abstraction, i.e., theory, representation and implementation (Halliday & Matthiessen 1999: 32; Matthiessen 1988; Matthiessen & Nesbitt 1996; Bateman 1997; Teich 1999).

The stratification model of meta-language into theory, representation and implementation was first introduced around 1980 in the process of developing Penman text-generator, and it had been more systematically explored and utilized for a period of time (1997—2005). The highest stratum of meta-language is the theory that means a semantic interpretation of language. Theory is realized or represented at the next lower level, and the representation is expected to be implemented in a programming language (Wu 2000). Theory is at a higher level, and it is a system of meanings or organization of the meaning description. The theoretical concepts are expected to be represented to have its linguistic realization. The concentration on the specific and concrete linguistic representation of theory is the center of this study. The different representing and implementing modes tell the sub-systemic functional linguistic branches apart under the grand framework of SFG, such as Fawcett and his Cardiff grammar.

2.2.2 A Corpus Approach to SFG

In the latest edition of *An Introduction to Functional Grammar*, Halliday and Matthiessen (2004: 29) comment on the relationship between SFG and the corpus:

As grammarians we have to be able to shift our perspective, observing now from the system standpoint and now from that of the text; and we have to be aware at which point we are standing at any time. This issue has been strongly foregrounded by the appearance of the computerized corpus. A corpus is a large collection of instances of spoken and written texts; the corpuses now available contain enough data to give significantly new insights into the grammar of English, provided the data can be processed and interpreted. But the corpus does not write the grammar for you, any more than the data from experiments in the behavior of light wrote *Newton's Opticks* for him; it has to be theorized. Writing a description of a grammar entails constant shunting between the perspective of the system and the perspective of the instance.

The comment is significant in guiding the corpus-concerned SFG research, and it can be concluded as follows: firstly, Halliday's constant shift of observational angle between system and instances provides the space for the standing point of corpus approach to SFG (shifting toward the instance pole increases more possibility of the support and participation of the corpus); secondly, the subsidiary, supportive and data-persuasive values of a corpus approach are confirmed, and, especially, the instrumental worth of the approach to penetrating into SFG and getting "significantly new" findings is acknowledged and approved in SFG research; thirdly, the corpus approach is preconditioned by the "processed and interpreted" data, namely, one aspect is that the data must be annotated to make meaning in corpus concordance, and the other is the methods of reading the retrieved lines and analyzing the statistical results; fourthly and most importantly, we must theorize on data, and theorization is an indispensable and necessary process in the way of finding new phenomena. All the statements above can be aspects of one problem, which means that the key to corpus approach to SFG is to set the position of corpus approach in the proper space between systems and instances. One of the preconditions for the resolution for the specific problems and general ones depends on finding the complementarities and resolving certain contradictions between SFG, the corpus, and CL. The incorporation of corpora and CL into SFG can be penetrated into through a specific comparison between the two disciplines. As for the approach to theorizing on language according to corpus observation, Halliday (2004a: 34) puts forward, "the corpus is fundamental to the enterprise of theorizing language".

Therefore, a corpus approach to SFG is fundamental because it is the means and instrument to fulfill the task of theorizing on language and linguistic phenomena, and it is a research on SFG from the opposite side of the traditional study. Let me cite a figure to illustrate the way of corpus penetration that is in the medium of the instantiation from system to instance.

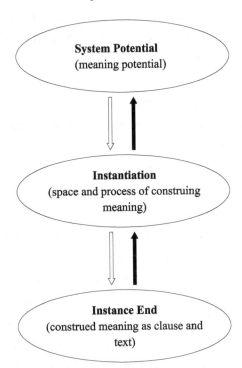

Figure 2-1   Illustration of Instantiation from Potential to Instance

The appearance of the huge corpora and their advanced technology makes the instance end (illustrated at the bottom of Figure 2-1) more plentiful and powerful. The new characteristics of the instances discovered by CL should not be ignored in SFG because theory comes out of the linguistic observation on linguistic data and should go back to data again for attestation and further exploration. The traditional research into SFG after Halliday and other scholars has two main trends: the first is to move from the pole of metafunctions towards that of instances, which starts from the pole of metafunctions; the second is to reason within theory with few instances or no instances. The shortcoming of the two traditional ways above is that the research is confined within the present framework of SFG, and it is hard to go beyond to rethink some problems within SFG guided by the set theoretical framework. Though some sporadic instances may indicate something, it is not dependable. Both the traditional ways referred to above are from systems to instances by means of instantiation, as is shown by the white arrows in Figure 2-1, that is to mean, theory is used to observe texts. The corpus way starts out of texts and reaches theory through instantiation, as is shown by the black arrows in Figure 2-1. Two different ways can lead to different methods and findings in their application. In general, the traditional research of SFG emphasizes the guidance and source of the systemic functional theory in reasoning on linguistic data, and it is a theory-to-language way, while the corpus approach is a language-to-theory one. Therefore, the corpus approach has its unique way that deserves special attention. A better apprehension of corpus approach is preceded by a comprehensive knowledge of the corpus and its methodology and theory. The traditional way is familiar to us, and here the corpus way is what is expected to concentrate on.

What is the corpus approach to SFG? What is the method of the corpus approach? How are data annotated? What are the inter-relationships between the theories of SFG and corpus linguistics? For those questions, neither Halliday nor Matthiessen has given a clear definition. Before trying to learn how to find an appropriate corpus approach from the instance end, we'd better get an outline of the corpus and corpus linguistics. Answering all the questions begins with more learning of the corpus and corpus linguistics.

2.2.2.1 The Corpus, an Objective Tool in Linguistic Description and Attestation

As for the question of what a corpus is, each scholar has his or her unique understanding and emphasizes different aspects from his or her own perspective.

Sinclair (1991: 13-20) gives a penetrative definition from the angle of establishing a corpus, claiming that a corpus is a collection of the naturally occurring linguistic texts chosen to characterize a state or variety of a language. Features of linguistic data are as follows: electronic, permitted (permitted copyright), designed (representative), spoken & written, typical, temporal and large enough (the scale of capacity of a corpus). Sinclair's concept of a corpus emphasizes two opinions: the first is that a corpus is a well-designed and registers-balanced linguistic database, and the other is that the function of a corpus is for linguistic description and particular linguistic phenomenon study. A similar definition is given as follows, "It should be added that computer corpora are rarely haphazard collections of textual material: They are generally assembled with particular purposes in mind, and are often assembled to be (informally speaking) representative of some language or text type" (Leech 1992: 116). Like Sinclair, Leech emphasizes the careful preparation of corpus materials to keep the linguistic data balanced in register and representative of the research purpose. Halliday (2004a) specifies the characteristics of the corpus and believes that a corpus should be characteristic of: 1) being made up of naturally occurring language; 2) being readily available and easy to get access to; 3) being large enough to provide a significant sample of the least common structures we are interested in; 4) being drawn from the specified genres. Halliday defines the corpus in three considerations: function, applicability and objectivity. McEnery & Andrew (2001: 29) regards the corpus as the basis for a form of empirical linguistics with four qualities: sampling and representativeness, finite size, machine-readable form and a standard reference. Neale (2002: 194) understands the corpus in another perspective, "I shall define a corpus as a large body of text instances which has been collected according to defined principles, and which can be examined and queried to assist the researcher in testing hypotheses about language in use".

Neale foregrounds the attesting function of the corpus in linguistic research, suggesting that the corpus is instrumental in testing linguistic research, meanwhile she supports a balanced corpus set up with certain principles. While, of course, her definition is very narrow because it is closely related with her special research in Cardiff grammar. Halliday and Matthiessen (2004: 29) are enthusiastic about the corpus and believe that a corpus is a large collection of instances of spoken and written texts. Both of them hold the view that corpora available contain enough data to give significantly new insights into the grammar of English, provided the data can be processed and interpreted. Furthermore, Matthiessen's (2006: 107) *archives* represents the informal collection of data that happen to be handy while his concept of *corpus* refers to more careful samplings of language. He makes the point of the selectiveness of linguistic data, and his distinctive confinement shows his views on the quality of the corpus, that is, the careful design of the corpus to keep objective in the selections of the registers of linguistic data. Teubert (2007: 140) adds that a corpus is "a collection of naturally occurring language texts in electronic form, often compiled according to specific design criteria and typically containing many millions of words". He emphasizes the corpus design and scale, both of which are closely related to the representativeness of the corpus data that ensures the objectivity of the study based on the corpus (or corpus-driven).

All the definitions above are given from a variety of perspectives. It is concluded from all those concepts that the most basic quality of a corpus is objective and instrumental in linguistic description and attestation. The objectivity is ensured by the choices of a large amount of the real linguistic data from different genres with a presupposed proportion. (Of course, I do not oppose the random corpus because the research based on or driven by the random corpus is also objective for a special research.) The corpus serves as a tool, through which we can see more linguistic data than what we can observe by other means and look farther than what we can do in a single text, part(s) of a text or several texts. These two instrumental functions can be compared to the ones of a microscope and a telescope, both of which provide the instrument and means to observe the magic microcosm and macrocosm that we cannot see in the usual way. The instrument with its attached methods and theory must be made clear before we go on to consider the compatibility of the application of the tool of the corpus to SFG research. The methodology and theory attached to the corpus are what corpus linguistics deal with.

2.2.2.2 CL, a Way and Method in Linguistic Study

CL is a subdivision of linguistic study based on corpora and a new approach to penetrating into linguistic description in a distinctive way from those of the other linguistics. Whether in the corpus-based approach or the corpus-driven one, it expands the scope of linguistic study and makes the research more objective and representative with huge data and advanced concordance than that based on reasoning on the fewer researchers' subjective and introspective linguistic data and the related reasoning.

Other different ideas about the quality of corpora and CL exist. McEnery (2001: 2) states that CL is not a branch of linguistics like syntax, semantics or sociolinguistics, but a methodology or approach that can be applied to many aspects of linguistic enquiry and used in almost any area of linguistics. Meanwhile, he emphasizes that CL gives researchers a different approach to and a distinctive perspective of the study on language, and CL should constitute an area of linguistics or one of the series of areas of linguistics. The core idea of his two-faceted definition is that CL is, in linguistic study, a tool that itself needs to be further expanded, advanced and penetrated into like other linguistic disciplines. Renouf (2005:2) gives a somewhat distinctive concept of CL, namely, CL is, by definition, a branch of linguistics and the study of language. Its primary objective is to discover the facts of the language. It represents a particular approach to linguistics that consists of the empirical observation and analysis of authentically-occurring texts. He confirms the disciplinary position of CL, as well as its methodological and instrumental quality. Teubert (2007: 59-80) sees CL from another perspective distinctive from the ones above. He thinks that CL treats language as a social phenomenon, and the focus of CL is the study of meaning that is defined as usage and paraphrase.

It can be concluded that the corpus is a tool objective in linguistic description and attestation, and CL is a methodology and an angle from which language is shown different from the one by the traditional ways. The corpus is the way through which theories and technological means of CL are realized and, in turn, it is guided and explored into by CL. Generally speaking, CL describes language and attests research through the corpus, and what CL deals with is the meaning in the form of usage and its paraphrase.

2.3 Questions to Be Answered

Most scholars have confirmed the value of the corpus and CL in the research of SFG, but their views of the incorporation of the corpus and CL into SFG are distinctive. The two tendencies of scholars are corpus-based and corpus-driven. The strong point of the corpus-based SFG study is that it both follows the theories in SFG and cites instances from corpora, combining the theories found in SFG and linguistic data in corpora. The great feature of the corpus-based approach to SFG is the theorization on linguistic data from corpora under the theoretical framework of SFG, and thus the approach makes the research more objective and penetrative. Meanwhile, the annexation presents some problems in the study.

The literature concerned tells that the corpus-based approach is too SFG-heavy to proceed, in which the corpus is regarded only as an instance resource for examples to support a theory or linguistic phenomenon. The way pays little attention to the ideas and methods of CL for reference. What is more, it proposes the pure manual annotation of the linguistic information of SFG at the clausal level, and all materials are explained under the framework of SFG. Though more grammatical information can be marked in linguistic data, it is difficult to form a corpus because a pure manual annotation is labor-intensive and time-consuming. Besides, most corpus-based researches are based on a small number of handy or pre-arranged texts, and Matthiessen names his small collection of texts *archives* instead of a corpus. Therefore, most corpus-based studies are not the ones as expected, and the corpus-based way is more instances-based actually. The corpus-based approach is thus too SFG-heavy to go on in an objective and efficient way.

On the other hand, the corpus-driven approach is too CL-heavy but SFG-light, and it pays little attention to the discovered regularities and theories in SFG. In the approach, researchers are suspicious of the objectivity and the truth of the theories found in SFG, and they believe only the rules and regularities concluded from linguistic data in the corpus. The corpus-driven research on SFG is simply both an attestation of the theories of SFG and conclusion from the pure linguistic data with little theoretical consideration and reference in fact. It is thus much too limited in linguistic discovery. In addition to the limitation of the attestation and conclusion purely on data, its suspicion is a great obstacle in finding more penetrative things with efficiency. Only observation and theorization on data are more or less superficial if there is no sound theoretical basis or guidance. The corpus-driven one is not the appropriate way to incorporate the corpus and CL into SFG either.

The inadequateness of two approaches calls for a reconsideration of incorporating the corpus and CL into SFG. In general, the rethinking consists of three questions. In which way do they use corpora, corpus-based, corpus-driven, both or neither? In the third edition of *An Introduction to Functional Grammar* (2004), corpus application is very preliminary, a kind of informal and example-citing use, in which Halliday and Matthiessen retrieve the corpus for examples that suit their purposes. Therefore, it is hard to be corpus-related. Is there a systemic discussion on the role of the corpus in SFG study? What is the specific study about the mutual acceptance or recognition in both theory and application to support the corpus approach in SFG? What is more, the annotation of the corpus under the framework of SFG is still manual; can the bottleneck of the growth of the corpus in SFG research be broken by a new approach?

Answering all the questions above depends on a systemic penetration into the relationships between SFG and CL in both theory and application. Furthermore, the corpus or CL approach to SFG study is expected to be based on the systemic theoretical modification and modeling to seek for a properly-expanded new area of SFG, and the corpus way in SFG is wanted to be guided under certain modified framework and the concrete applicable models. Before coming to the new incorporation of the corpus and CL into SFG, it is necessary to conduct comparable and contrastive studies on the two branches.

Chapter Three

Commonalities and Disparities Between SFG and CL

Though the linguistic frontiersmen like Thompson, Tucker, Neal, Matthiessen, etc. have already started the exploration a long time before, the incorporation of the corpus and CL approach and ideas into SFG still has a long way to go, because some basic problems still exist for further consideration and solution. Specifically speaking, the methodological problems are: How and in what way is the corpus applied in SFG study? In which way are the raw linguistic data annotated, manually or automatically? Whether the corpus-based or corpus-driven approach is the only way, and if only, which is right or better? To be specific, the theoretical problems are: What are the value and position of the ideas and means of CL in the research of SFG? To what extent are both the linguistic disciplines compatible? How do the methods of CL melt into the system framework of SFG? Answering all the questions listed needs a systematic study of the methods and theories of both SFG and CL.

3.1 Commonalities Between SFG and CL

Mair (2009) proposes that the elaboration on the commonalities, complementarities and disparities between CL and sociolinguistics is the basis and pre-condition of the corpus-based sociolinguistic research when looking for the role of corpus evidence in the study of the sociolinguistic variation and change. No exception is the exploration into the relationships between CL and SFG. Originally, Halliday inherited the central ideas of the linguistics of London School from his teacher, Firth, and developed SFG. Hallidayan SFG is thus founded on empiricism and follows the attached epistemology.

3.1.1 Philosophical Basis

Since the emergence of philosophy, there has come out two mainstreams, empiricism and rationalism, from which two different linguistic schools have come into view. Halliday typically represents the British empiric basis from his tutor, Firth, the founder of British linguistics. In England, there is a long tradition of philosophical empiricism developed by Bacon, Locke, Newton and Hume. That empiricism has greatly influenced the linguistics in the UK, and Firth has founded the contemporary linguistics in his country. Literally speaking, empiricism holds the view that all knowledge is derived from the sense experience. The main ideas of empiricism are developed and made concrete in Bacon's scientific experimentalism that emphasizes three aspects: empirical, instrumental and applicable. Linguistics, especially the linguistic research in the UK cannot avoid being affected and learns a lot from it. Empiricism comes to serve as a fundamental view in linguistics, in which sense experience is the ultimate source of language learning. It is thus concluded that the experience in the inner and outside worlds is the only source of meaning and language acquisition. The meaning we exchange through language is the one construed by lexico-grammar of a language in certain context because experience happens in certain context. Therefore, meaning comes out of the experience in the world and is construed by a language in certain context. Besides, the great specific influence of empiricism and its epistemology on SFG is that all linguistic study in Hallidayan linguistics starts from the concrete, real and natural language use. As a result, the empirical research methodology is deeply rooted in SFG and shows itself in many aspects of the SFG research. SFG thus shows such features as follows:

1) what SFG focuses on are the linguistic models;

2) patterns of construing meaning through language are the core of SFG,

namely, the relationship between meaning and its realization of linguistic form;

3) the foundation for the research in SFG is the really and naturally occurring data of language, not the one from the heads of armchair linguists;

4) delicate and accurate research is advocated and ensured by the statistical means applied to linguistic data;

5) research in SFG should thus be concrete, comprehensive and objective;

6) it is applicable and necessary to introduce the corpus and its research methodology to SFG.

The realization of the six features above depends on the statistics of the frequency (or relative frequency) of linguistic features in texts. Halliday (2004: 58) puts forward: "A language is a meaning potential, one that is open-ended: the grammatics has to explain how this meaning potential is exploited, and also how it can be enlarged. And this is where I see a complementarity between systemic theory and corpus linguistics." The reason for Halliday to propose such ideas is that the instantiation of meaning potential can be made more concrete, delicate and accurate through a corpus way. Besides, the corpus is a more objective and efficient means of abridging the gap between system and instances. The application of the corpus and CL to SFG research depends on exploring the complementarities of both disciplines, and it starts with an exploration into the commonalities and disparities between SFG and CL.

The linguistic ideas of Firth have been greatly affected by Saussure and Malinowski. Firth inherits Saussure's linguistic ideas of a system of systems and extends the concepts of system and structure. Firth stresses that the paradigmatic relationship is the most basic one in system and the syntagmatic one is shown as a chain at bottom in structure. His opinion on paradigmatic relationship was pioneering at that time, which is further emphasized and advanced by his student Halliday. Firth (1957) points out that the central topic of linguistics is the study of meaning of language in natural use in certain context, which has originated from Malinowski's ideas. Saussure believes that meaning comes out of lexical syntagmatic position in the sentence structure, and later on, the explanation of meaning is developed by Firth, whose opinion is that meaning is produced in a word's company it keeps. The company contains more meaning than that generated only from structure. The company of a word is a kind of collocation in certain context, which suggests that meaning contains not only the one produced in structure, but the one created by the surrounding linguistic or non-linguistic environment.

Specifically, Firth's ideas of meaning are concerned about both the meaning originating from the position in language structure, and the one from the closely-related context outside, which are made more concrete by his proposition of the typical linguistic context involving both inner textual relationships and inner linguistic context. Halliday concentrates on the system and function of language. He emphasizes the paradigmatic relationships of figures and makes the point that meaning is, instead of the company a linguistic unit keeps or collocation, a kind of choice from a meaning potential. That is to say, meaning is more paradigmatic than syntagmatic, and the true nature of system is paradigmatic. Syntagmatic system is the structure deriving from the construction of a figure and originates from the choice of constituents or elements of figures. Furthermore, the choice of meaning from linguistic potential characterizes that language is probabilistic in nature. Wei, Li and Pu. (2005: 1) comment on the relationships between SFG and CL as follows: concerning the disciplinary character, CL belongs to the school of empiricism on philosophical ground. CL agrees with SFG, and both ideas come from Firth. Observed from above, language is regarded as a social phenomenon in both SFG and CL, and language study is based on language use and naturally-occurring texts.

Firth's and Halliday's linguistic ideas prove themselves empiric. Both of them have proposed their ideas from the perspective of language in certain context, that is, language in use in the real life and naturally-occurring language. They start their research from the linguistic empiric facts and induce what they observe in a way from particular to general. The probabilistic quality of language proposed by Halliday is derived from both the observation and the frequency counting of natural language.

3.1.2 Meaning and Its Representation

Both SFG and CL treat language as a social phenomenon and base their research on language use and naturally-occurring texts. In SFG, language is a meaning potential resource to construct social reality and interpersonal relationship, in which meaning is construed by the choices from the lexico-grammatical network in language, and a text is the result of the choices of lexico-grammar in certain context. Meaning construction of the surrounding world (including inner world) and textual relationship is affected by the context that determines the mode and characteristics of the choice network of lexico-grammar and reality construction; meanwhile, the feature that the meaning construction is confined by context reflects that meaning is social in nature. What is more, the sociality of meaning decided by context is realized in the form of the probabilistic variations of the lexico-grammatical choices from the meaning potential.

Therefore, it is concluded that meaning construction in SFG is socially probabilistic. Correspondingly, concerning the sociality of meaning, CL shares the same views, "We take the view that language is a social behavior and meaning a social phenomenon. By this we mean that language is more than an individual possession or ability, that language 'exists' because of its life in social interaction, that meaning is shaped and negotiated in social interaction and that meaning must be studied with due recognition of its social setting" (Yallop 2004: 41-42). The views in CL show that meaning is created and modified in men's social reaction; therefore, meaning is social in nature because it is men's social actions created in the social interactions between men. The quality of the social characteristics of meaning is further elaborated by Teubert, and he (2004: 97-98) specifies the social features of meaning in CL, commenting that language is regarded as a social phenomenon in CL. His social meaning of language contains three points: firstly, meaning is a social phenomenon that can be discussed by members of a discourse community; secondly, there is no right or wrong secret formula, neither in natural language nor in a formal calculus, which contains the meaning of a word or phrase; thirdly, meaning is what can be communicated verbally. The three points of Teubert can be specified in the following suggestions: 1) meaning is the social product, specifically, the product of language use in society; 2) meaning can be conveyed in oral and written forms; 3) meaning is not decided by form, but closely related to society; 4) meaning is the result of negotiation between members of the social community, and there is no standard for deciding on whether a meaning construing is right or wrong; 5) the carrier of meaning is language. The features of meaning in CL demonstrate the common views on the construction of meaning in the form of language in texts and contexts. The quality of meaning can be further testified and made more concrete in how meaning is processed in CL, "How does corpus linguistics deal with meaning? Meaning, as has been said before, is in the discourse. But how do we look for it there? How do we find it? There are two main aspects to meaning. Meaning is usage and paraphrase. Usage and paraphrase reflect the two ways we deal with language" (Teubert 2004: 127). The views on meaning above show that meaning is the real language use, and the text is the basic unit for meaning paraphrase in CL. In addition, the idea of meaning as usage and paraphrase indicates that meaning performs the social function of interactions between men in community. In SFG, meaning is the instance in the form of lexico-grammar chosen from the meaning potential, that is, the clause. To be specific, meaning is constructed out of the instantiation of linguistic meaning potential and into the figure that is represented as clause by lexico-grammar. It can thus be said that the minimum of unit at the level of meaning creation in language use is clause in text (of course in certain context), which is mutually shared by both SFG and CL. The idea of construing meaning in the sociality of language, text and context is the common ground shared by both branches of linguistics.

3.1.3 Systemic Probability of Language

As is stated above, the construction of reality through language is a dynamic process related to context. Halliday (1992) regards lexico-grammar of language as an elastic space between the material dimension and the conscious one. The elasticity is represented, in construing meaning, as the variation of probability of choices from the meaning potential pole. Furthermore, the meaning potential is essentially a paradigmatic system, namely, a selective system with permissions in SFG (Halliday 1993a: 94). Both ideas show that meaning is a probabilistic choice from system, which is also shared by CL. The paradigmatic quality of system determines that the linguistic instantiation of meaning from potential to instance is probabilistic in nature. In CL, meaning is usage that is realized in the form of lexico-grammatical choices, and we can thus conclude that meaning is choice. The dynamic process in which lexico-grammar constructs reality consists of two parts: firstly, context determines the sociality of a lexico-grammatical choice; secondly, there is still the freedom of a lexico-grammatical choice under certain context. Both contextual determination and elastic construction demonstrate that language is probabilistic in nature and linguistic potential system is a probabilistic system of choice. Frequency in text is the instantiation of probability in the system. Halliday (2005: 45) comments on choice and systemic probability as follows:

A linguistic system is inherently probabilistic in nature...Obviously, to interpret language in probabilistic terms, the grammar (that is, the theory of grammar, the grammatics) has to be paradigmatic: it has to be able to represent language as choice, since probability is the probability of "choosing" (not in any conscious sense, of course) one thing rather than another. Firth's concept of "system", in the "system / structure" framework, already modeled language as choice. Once you say "choose for polarity: positive or negative?", or "choose for tense: past or present or future?", then each of these options could have a probability value attached.

The probabilistic nature of language derived from SFG is represented in the paradigmatic system, and this feature determines that systemic choice originates from the constituents. The determination is represented by lexis or limited grammar that can be represented by lexical association. Therefore, it is thus considered that the systemic choice in SFG starts with lexical choice. In CL, lexical choice is the most basic unit, and lexical preference is essential in CL, in which the concordance and tagging in the corpus are lexical or lexically-patterned (regex). Whether the research is into phraseology, register variation of texts or into linguistic features in CL, the foregrounding probability profile of the linguistic phenomena is built out of the probability pattern of the lexical choices that can be further combined and modified to realize a purpose at a higher grammatical level. It can be concluded that both branches of linguistics share the same probabilistic views on the realization of the probability profile. Specifically, in both branches, language is probabilistic in nature and the probability profile is realized by counting the relative frequency of certain linguistic feature. In addition, the most basic unit in building the probability profile is the lexical unit.

3.2 Disparities Between SFG and CL

3.2.1 Theory and Methodology

"SFG is essentially a theory of language; CL is essentially a method of investigating language." (Thompson 2006:1) SFG is theory-heavy and it theorizes on texts. In SFG, the system of language is a very complicated network interlocked closely by a scale of delicacy of ranks and levels as is dealt with in Chapters One and Two. Specifically, SFG deals with clause through three distinctive and synchronic metafunctions, each of which has a micro-system because the language system in SFG is coped with from the perspective of function that a language plays. Description of language in SFG is theoretically heavy and thick. Besides, SFG moves further out of language itself and shows the great concern about the non-linguistic context that includes both situational contexts and socio-cultural ones. Theory is established by theorizing on texts in SFG, and the deriving method of SFG is thus the theorization on the observation of the linguistic features (or statistical results of the relative frequency of the features) of a text or several ones. The mode of research in SFG is grammar-driven or theory-driven, and all the study goes on under certain theoretical framework. Therefore, SFG is, in essence, a theoretical framework that needs to be expanded and perfected with further study, but the orientation of the theory cannot be changed. To be specific, the research in SFG is expected to be done under the framework of linguistic system and function in certain context. SFG is clearly orientated, and its theory is one-dimensional although its application is multi-dimensional. In addition to theorizing on texts, SFG can be dated back to construing meaning out of lexico-grammar. So it can be concluded that SFG is grammatics-driven and it is thus derived that once a research is begun in SFG, it is SFG-driven.

As is stated in Section 2.2.3.2, there has been no ultimate judgment on the concept of CL. Some scholars think that it is an independent discipline, while others not. Kennedy (1998: 1) gives a vague definition to CL and thinks CL is a scholarly enterprise concerned with the compilation and analysis of corpora. McEnery and Wilson (1996: 1) foregrounds the methodological function of CL, saying it is the study of language based on the examples of the real life language use and a methodology rather than an aspect of language requiring explanation or description. Stubbs (1996: 231) stresses the theory-light quality of CL and states that CL has as yet only very preliminary outlines of a theory which can relate individual texts to text corpora. Hunston (2002: 3) refers to CL as an instrument to process linguistic data via software packages to show frequency, phrase structure and collocation. A more comprehensive and general definition is given by Tognini-Bonelli (2001: 1): "We have, so far, assumed that corpus linguistics is a methodology rather than an independent branch of linguistics. This view, however, is not shared by all scholars. For example, it has been argued that corpus linguistics 'goes well beyond this methodological role' and has become an independent 'discipline'." We are not sure whether it is an independent discipline or not, but we can know that it is a methodology applied in linguistic research. Specifically speaking, the methodology is represented as a tool to exploit the large amount of linguistic data in corpora to theorize on observation of the data, attest theories and suppositions and propose revelations. Whether it is a corpus-based approach or corpus-driven one in CL, it is theory-light or neutral but linguistic data-dependent. The instrumental method of CL in the linguistic research is widely applied in most research in different linguistic schools because CL provides naturally-occurring proofs and less pre-supposed theory intervention. Therefore, it can be said that CL is essentially an empiric method of linguistic research at least.

3.2.2 Meaning

In SFG, meaning is studied in both linguistic and non-linguistic contexts. The nature of meaning is construed by language, and the construing process is greatly influenced by the situational context and the socio-cultural one. Deconstruction of meaning abides by the same conditions of both language and two kinds of contexts. So the meaning in SFG is both language-partial and context-partial. From the perspective of language, the unit of meaning is construed into figures (containing participant, process and circumstance) that are realized by lexico-grammar of language in the form of clauses. Text is the complete form of meaning, which represents the experience ahead of linguistic construction. The complete meaning analysis starts from clauses in a text with consideration of the contexts in which the text is construed. Therefore, meaning is both linguistic and non-linguistic in SFG. In addition, meaning is probabilistic in nature from the perspective of meaning realization. The whole system of language is a meaning potential, and the realization or construction of meaning in the linguistic form is a choice from the meaning potential. The probability of choice is determined by the contextual configuration. It is concluded from above that the character of meaning is linguistic, construing, contextual (non-linguistic) and probabilistic.

However, meaning in CL is the instance usage of language. The meaning in CL is bi-dimensional: meaning is the usage to a speaker, but the paraphrase to a hearer. The meaning of the same unit is distinctive for a speaker and a hearer, and thus it is the communicative role that determines the meaning scope. Meaning in CL is essentially verbal though it recognizes the social phenomenal meaning. Teubert (2004: 97-99) believes the dynamic and unstable quality of meaning by claiming that meaning is something customized in the constitutions of all members of a community, "Meaning is what can be communicated verbally. If you do not know what apophthegm means, you can ask your fellow members of the English discourse community". Besides emphasizing the usage form of meaning in the verbal communication, Teubert moves further to the existence of meaning in a linguistic form, that is, the discourse. Here the discourse is different from the text in SFG, which is a single instantiation of experience in the linguistic form of a single text or several specific texts. "Corpus linguistics studies languages on the basis of discourse. English discourse is the totality of texts produced, over centuries, by the members of the English discourse community." (Teubert 2004: 100) Meaning of a linguistic unit is not the one specific in a single text, but a semantic prosody in all texts produced over history in which there is a unit. Meaning in corpora is more general in CL than in SFG. Meaning in CL is more observational, while, in SFG, it is more analytical. The observation is horizontal because the meaning search or concordance is closely related with the company a linguistic unit keeps in texts, and thus it concentrates on collocation, namely, the relationships between collocates. It can be generalized that meaning is verbal, horizontal in collocation, speaker or hearer-determined, discourse-crossing and semantic prosody-described in CL.

In SFG and CL, meaning is penetrated into from different perspectives, and meaning thus shows distinctive aspects in either linguistics. The most distinguishing question is whether meaning is paradigmatically chosen from the meaning potential of language in a probability profile determined by register, or it is syntagmatically derived from collocations of all discourse in history identified by the company a meaning unit keeps.

3.2.3 Context

Halliday inherits the contextual ideas from Firth, whose opinion on context is greatly influenced by Malinowski. The context of a text in SFG is extended into a greater non-linguistic environment that affects the linguistic meaning and function in a text. Hasan specifies the concept of context into the contextual configuration that consists of tenor, field and mode, each of which defines the possible register in which a meaning is construed. Halliday (2004a: 27-28) relates context to register, which is similar to genre of a text:

> However, research has shown that texts vary systematically according to contextual values: texts vary according to the nature of the contexts they are used in. Thus recipes, weather forecasts,

stock market reports, rental agreements, e-mail messages, inaugural speeches, service encounters in the local deli, news bulletins, media interviews, tutorials sessions…and all the other innumerable text types we meet in life are all ways of using language in different contexts. Looked at from the system pole of the cline of instantiation, they can be interpreted as registers.

A register is a functional variety of language (Halliday 1978), or the patterns of instantiation of the overall system associated with a given type of context (a situation type) in origin. Those patterns of instantiation show up as adjustments in the systemic probabilities of language in a quantitative way, in other sense, the patterns of instantiation result in a register that can be represented as a particular setting of systemic probabilities. For example, the future tense is very much more likely to occur in weather forecasts than it is in stories (for examples of quantitative profiles of registers, see Matthiessen 2002). In SFG, the term register is the functional variety of language and the contextual values associated with such a functional variety (Martin 1992; Matthiessen 1993). Though inheriting from Firth and Malinowski, Halliday's understanding of context is mainly the result of the realization of the contextual affection of elements in linguistic functions.

In CL, context is more one-dimensional, and it is more linguistic than contextual. Firth proposes that we know a word by the company it keeps, and the company here refers to the linguistic context in which a node is explained. A contextual company of a key word is not all the collocates around it in the retrieved lines, but the ones with high frequency and typicality. To be specific, the linguistic context of a node in concordance lines is named semantic prosody or semantic preference. Semantic prosody refers to the contextual word pattern that shows the accustomed collocation or attraction of the collocates similar in meaning that permeates the semantic atmosphere of the node, and semantic prosody is classified into three types: negative, neutral and positive ones (Sinclair 1991: 74-75; Louw 1993: 156-159; Stubbs 1996: 176). The decoding of the meaning of a node under a linguistic context in CL is more general and comprehensive; on the other hand, it can be said that the explanation is vague, abstract, confined and inflexible. Meaning in CL is confined to the set semantic one that can only be explained by the surrounding linguistic units. While in SFG, meaning is deconstructed from both the linguistic context (including the role of a constituent plays in a figure, the other constituents in a figure, the figures around the researched figure and the whole text) and the non-linguistic context attached to the target text or discourse. The meaning in SFG is more specific and concrete, and it contains both the one deconstructed from the linguistic context like the meaning decoded in CL, and the one from the non-linguistic one. Though both the linguistic branches read meaning from linguistic context, the deconstructing mode of meaning in SFG differs greatly from the decoding way of meaning in CL because of either respective understanding of context. The mode in SFG is to find the meaning of a unit through its relationships with other units in a text and contexts, while the decoding way of meaning in CL seeks for the common semantic features of the surrounding collocates of high frequency. Therefore, the meaning decoded in CL way is somewhat distracted from the specific meaning in the specified retrieved line because of the context quality of the retrieved lines. It can be thus reasoned that the linguistic context of a unit is the semantic prosody or preference, and this kind of context determines the meaning features decoded in CL.

3.3 Synergies and Complementarities Between SFG and CL

Though there are great differences in understanding and describing linguistic phenomena between both branches, there is still the value to explore into the synergies and complementarities between them because CL provides a new distinctive perspective and an instrument to watch a large number of naturally-occurring linguistic texts. Some linguists even believe that the corpus linguistic methodology is both a telescope and a microscope for linguistic observation, through which we can see more faraway and observe more minute things than by reading a single text or several texts. With the development of modern science and technology, the linguistic research becomes multi-dimensional to a larger extent.

The tendency of mutual reference and merging makes SFG and CL come closer. Concerning the relationship between SFG and CL, Thompson (2006: 1) comments, "SFL (systemic functional grammar) is increasingly concerned with methods of qualifying linguistic features, and CL is becoming more intent on developing theories to account for its findings. Many practitioners, whatever their backgrounds, have a sympathy for both approaches and see them as complementary rather than in opposition". Many linguists have been engaged in the direction. The research of Hoey (2006) and Hunston (2006) mediates between SFG and CL to try to explain, under the framework of SFG, the instances from corpus concordance. Both of them thus extended the scope of CL to concern not only what collocations are, but also how and why. Their research on the mutual relationship between instance and corpora is under certain social context, and it tries to find the compatibility between the description based on large-scaled linguistic data in CL and the theoretical description in SFG. Tucker (2006) tries to explain, in the theoretical framework of SFG, the phraseological instances, or semi-fixed phrases retrieved from corpora. Stubbs's approach is corpus-driven, trying to build a sociolinguistic mode out of the instantiated co-occurring pattern from retrieved linguistic data in psycholinguistic mechanism from corpora. Neale's approach is also corpus-driven, and she applies corpora to the transitivity in SFG and gives a supplement to the present transitivity classifications. Sharoff builds a model of words for the realization of communicative purpose out of the systemic network of lexical choices in SFG.

Halliday (2008: 12) shows great concern for the complementarities between SFG and CL/corpora in his recent work *Complementarities in Language,* and he approves of the way Hoey proposes. Hoey, referred to in the literature, is a corpus-driven supporter, and he emphasizes the contribution made by patterns in lexis to the coherence and the organization of a text. Specifically speaking, Hoey shows how the selection of lexical items manifest the progressive unfolding of the discourse to understand the essential nature and underlying message of a text, and what is more, to assess and explain its effect. While the key to Hoey's approach to the nature of text is to find "patterns in lexis", which is surely corpus-dependent.

Halliday (2008: 13) comments on Hoey's linguistic way, "What I saw as another complementarity in language, that between language as system and language as text...I feel it is important to refer to the complementarity in these terms, 'language as system' and 'language as text', in order to stress that these are two aspects of one single phenomenon—not two different phenomena, as is implied if you use a simple duality like 'language and text', or 'langue and parol'. System and text are one and the same phenomenon; the system is simply the potential that is **instantiated** in every moment of discourse...System and text are related by the vector of 'instantiation'". Halliday confirms that Hoey's corpus-based study on discourse nature is complementary to system, for a lexical penetration into discourse through the corpus is a section in the continuum with the corpus and system as the two ends, which is made clearer earlier by saying "a good grammar book ought to locate these (paradigmatic words in thesauri) in their place in a network of grammatical systems, but that still requires more corpus-based grammatical research" (Halliday 2008: 27). Concerning the syntagmatic collocation and the paradigmatic choice of system, Halliday (2008) and Sinclair (2003) believe that collocation is a formal relation among lexical items that is manifested in quantitative terms, and the extent to which the probability of a word is perturbed by the environment in which it occurs, and specifically, by other words occurring around it, or within certain distance at least. The nature and extent of this distance remain to be empirically determined by a span of four or five lexical words on either side of the node. Both Halliday and Sinclair believe the syntagmatic collocation and the paradigmatic choice of system form a crossroads at which the latter's profile of probability of choice is affected by the former. But Halliday's opinion on the influential factors of the probability of the paradigmatic choice of system goes beyond Sinclair's collocational span on either side of the node, and it is more concerned with the lexical inherent probability and the context of a text. "The key concept was that of lexically conditioned probabilities: a word has an inherent (unconditioned) probability of occurrence in a text, shown by its ranking in the order of word frequency; but this will be perturbed (conditioned) by the particular textual environment, and specifically by the other words that occur in its immediate neighbourhood." Halliday (2008: 40) The profile of probability of lexico-grammar is established by the frequency of lexico-grammar in a text, and Halliday (2008: 42-43) once comments, "Both lexical and grammatical frequencies are of course affected by features of the surrounding discourse. They are conditioned 'from above', by the choice of register (the text type, or functional variety); and they are conditioned 'from round about' by their collocational and systemic environment. Taken all together, the pattern of lexical and grammatical frequencies defines the probability profile of the lexico-grammatical stratum as a whole. This is an important feature of a language". It is thus concluded that CL is a way to establish the probability of the lexico-grammatical stratum in certain context (or inherent) through the concordance of lexico-grammatical frequency. "The corpus makes it possible to undertake quantitative studies not only of lexical items but also of terms in grammatical systems provided you can recognize these automatically." (Halliday 2008: 41) Grammar and lexis are a continuum, and grammar can be realized through the lexical pattern that can be edited as a regular expression for concordance; therefore, grammar is retrievable. *Pattern Grammar* (2000) by Hunston and Francis with the sub-title *A Corpus-driven Approach to the Lexical Grammar of English* demonstrates the lexical approach to grammar.

What has been described above demonstrates that the profile of probability of lexico-grammar can be established through the frequency (or relative frequency) of lexis. The relationship between SFG and CL is actually the one between lexis and grammar, both of which are the same continuum with the general systemic options at the grammatical end and the collocational regularities at the lexical end. The lexical concordance, including the regular expression concordances and the probability of lexico-grammar choice in system, is mutually constructed under certain context though both concentrate on different contexts. It is thus concluded from above that SFG and CL are synergic and complementary.

3.4 Summary

Both the corpus and CL serve as methodologies and make the research in SFG more concrete, operable, attestable and observable. To be specific, meaning in SFG can be made more expanded by observing the retrieved lines with more linguistic contexts. Meaning is studied in a fuller and broader sense beyond the one in the specified context in SFG. Besides, more linguistic contexts of a node in CL can make the meaning in SFG more specific and comparable with reference to the relative frequency of the meaning appearances in different linguistic contexts. Context is more observable and operable in the retrieved lines with the different spans set according to each distinctive research purpose. In addition, context research on the genre can be more deeply concentrated on in SFG with the help of corpus concordance and concordance techniques.

Though showing a lot of differences in meaning and context, SFG and CL are synergic and complementary in essence because those distinctions are mutually beneficial to each other. The common empiric basis and the probabilistic nature of language determine that there are enough commonalities to be explored to benefit the research in both SFG and CL.

Chapter Four

A Corpus-Supported Approach to SFG

The major idea in this book is the study of a corpus-supported approach to SFG, and it is neither completely SFG-featured nor CL-characteristic, nor a simple application or combination. The corpus and CL approach to SFG is a new branch related to the grand framework of SFG, and the approach has the unique characteristics that can provide a new perspective. The corpus-supported approach to SFG proposed in this study has its distinctive representing and implementing modes.

4.1 Reasons for a New Approach

As is suggested above, Halliday confirms the significance of the corpus in the study of lexico-grammar. Halliday's approach is corpus-based, and it emphasizes the annotated corpus data. He prefers a grammar-based corpus. Firstly Halliday (2008: 73-74) suggests that the corpus should be annotated or tagged at least because the corpus is lexis-preferable.

Whichever way we approach the study of lexico-grammar, progress from now on will depend on the corpus. The corpus is as much a resource for the grammarian as it is for the lexicologist; the problem is that, while the corpus is friendly to the lexicologist, it is notably unfriendly to the grammarian. This is partly because of the nature of the complementarity I have been talking about: lexical meaning is located much nearer the surface of language, so the written form of a word can (for the time being, at least) be used to define and delimit the object of study. Grammar is much more hidden from view; it is seldom that you can retrieve grammatical information directly from the written words. It will always take more effort to recognize and process grammatical phenomena. That said, however, it remains true that the way the corpus is designed also favours the lexicologist. It would be helpful to design a corpus so that some grammatical information could be built in to the basic plan: for example (thinking of English), tagging of some of the more easily recognized markers, like verbal and nominal deictics, paratactic and hypotactic conjunctions, with pattern-matching strategies for more complex categories such as non-finite aspect and voice; some more generalized procedures for concordancing, and for counting and indexing, based on such grammatical categories; some processing of intonation and rhythm for spoken text, and so on .

Matthiessen follows Halliday's annotated approach and establishes his *archives*, which consists of only 6,500 clauses. All data in *archives* are collected handily, that is, linguistic data are collected in a casual way, which is not completely Hallidayan. "Large-scale quantitative studies of the relative frequencies of grammatical features, and their combinations, can reveal much about the underlying probabilistic patterns in the language... Corpus linguists have asked us to work towards 'corpus-based grammars'; in order to be able to do this we have to ask them, in turn, to work towards a grammar-based corpus" (Halliday 2008: 75). Hallidayan approach, in general, is the grammar-based corpus in a large scale. Matthiessen's way is annotated, but not large-scaled. Besides, Matthiessen goes too far in the annotation because he fully annotates all grammar in the clauses in his *archives,* which is the reason for Matthiessen's less objective but more subjective research on the limited linguistic data. It is the time-consuming and labor-intensive manual annotation that confines the scale of a corpus. Though his *SysFan* annotating tool helps to reduce some troubles in annotation and statistics, it is manual in essence, which costs too much time and labor but achieves less. In the manual annotation, more grammatical information means more time and labor.

To annotate a large-scaled corpus costs a long time and a great amount of labor if annotation is purely manual. Is this tagging necessary? Or is it what Halliday expects? It is my opinion that the annotation in Matthiessen's way in his corpus-based research marks more grammar than what is necessary in the clauses of his *archives*. In addition to the shortcoming that much more time and labor produce fewer annotated data in the corpus, heavily-annotated grammar will probably affect the objectivity of the target linguistic data in the corpus because data have been biased before they are retrieved to tell the truth. It is not the way Halliday expects and proposes. Halliday (2008: 75) himself supports the tagged or somewhat-annotated corpus and contending: "It would be helpful to design a corpus so that some grammatical information could be built in to the basic plan: for example (thinking of English), tagging of some of the more easily recognized markers, like verbal and nominal deictics, paratactic and hypotactic conjunctions, with pattern-matching strategies for more complex categories such as non-finite aspect and voice; some more generalized procedures for concordancing, and for counting and indexing, based on such grammatical categories; some processing of intonation and rhythm for spoken text, and so on." Halliday proposes a simple tagging or annotation to try to keep the naturally-occurring linguistic data objective in order to make sure that the later result is well-founded.

However, the opposite tendency has become increasingly popular recently. Many developed tools are moving towards a more comprehensive SFG-based analysis, whose method is increasingly manual. A lot of annotating tools specially designed for systemic-functional analysis, e.g. Kasper's FUG parser[1] in 1988, Webster's functional grammar processor in 1993, O'Donnell's WAG system in 1994, Wu and Matthiessen's *SysFan* (part of SysAm that includes

---

[1] FUG parser stands for functional unification grammar representation parser. It is a computer program that transforms systemic network into functional unification grammar and marks the grammatical information in a text.

SysConc, SysRef, SysGraph and SysGloss[①]) in 2000 are the ones that serve as a workbench for manual annotation and relieve of some repeated troubles of statistics and marking on paper with a pen. Halliday and Matthiessen (1999: 553) believes it is not possible to analyze a large corpus automatically in terms of the system of PROCESS TYPE. The best possible way at present is to carry out very selective checking based on e.g. representative grammatical or lexical items. Matthiessen acknowledges that the corpus scale is confined by manual annotation and proposes a small-scaled selective corpus that is made as representative as possible. Later on, Matthiessen (2006: 109) explains that there is an inverse relationship: the more significant a system is in the organization of the lexico-grammar of a language, the harder it will be to automate the analysis. It shows that more grammar marking means less automatic process of linguistic data.

It is revealed that, in Halliday and Matthiessen's discussions, there are three contradictions in the corpus and methods of the application of CL to SFG: firstly, the contradiction between the very limited linguistic data in SFG, such as *archives,* and large-scaled corpora in CL like BNC, ICE, WebCorp; secondly, the contradiction between the annotated corpora under the framework of SFG and the clean corpora of texts, tagged ones or limitedly annotated ones in the traditional grammar; thirdly, the contradiction between manual annotation and the automatic tagging and annotating tendency.

The three contradictions confront us with a necessary reconsideration of the incorporation of the corpus and CL into the SFG search because both corpus-based and corpus-driven approaches fail to solve the contradictions appearing in the corpus-approach to SFG research at present. Therefore, it is essential to explore a new proper way to make the corpus and CL affect and support SFG research more positively and efficiently.

---

① They are series of software in which *SysFan* is integrated into the resource development environment SysAm where it not only interacts with SysConc but also with SysRef and other tools of SysAm such as SysGraph and SysGloss (Canzhong Wu).

4.2 Proposal for Corpus-Supported SFG

4.2.1 Proposal for a Corpus-Supported Approach to SFG

Before moving further on, some basic concepts would better be told apart. Concerning the application of the corpus to language research, there are two traditional ways: corpus-based and corpus-driven ones. With the distinctions of both approaches, it is necessary to come to Tognini-Bonelli's (2001) ideas on the differences between the corpus-based and corpus-driven investigations.

The major way in SFG is corpus-based, which advocates a detailed systemic and comprehensive annotation of the linguistic data in a corpus, e.g. Matthiessen (2006) and Wu (2000) with their *SysFan*, O'Donnell with his *Systemic Coder*, Judd and O'Halloran with their *Systemics*, Bateman with his *Grammar Explorer*. The Hallidayan (2008: 75) way is realized through the corpus-based grammatical research or a grammar-based corpus one by making the point, "Corpus linguists have asked us to work towards 'corpus-based grammars'; in order to be able to do this we have to ask them, in turn, to work towards a grammar-based corpus". A corpus-based one uses a corpus as a source to check researchers' intuition or examine the frequency and/or plausibility of language contained within a smaller data set, in which researchers do not question the pre-existing traditional descriptive units and categories. On the other hand, there are scholars that advocate a corpus-driven approach in SFG research.

As for the relationship between SFG and CL/corpora, Hunston and Francis' approach to pattern grammar (2000: 36) is in a corpus-driven way. A corpus-driven analysis tends to only use minimal theoretical presuppositions about grammatical structure (Baker 2006). A corpus-driven approach is a more inductive process and the corpus itself is the data and the patterns in it are noted as a way of expressing regularities in language. The elaborations above illustrate that the corpus-based one is theory-attesting, while the corpus-driven one, data-inducing. The former is preconditioned that the authority of a linguistic theory is not challenged and all the attestations of linguistic intuition must be worked out under the framework of that theory; the latter refuses to acknowledge little previously-existing theory and attempts to induce the linguistic data to make the observation results as objective as possible.

The three ensuing contradictions (reference to 4.1) deserve more reconsideration on Halliday's and Matthiessen's approaches. It is my opinion that both corpus-based and corpus-driven approaches go to extreme: a corpus-driven way deviates from the theory-heavy quality of SFG, doubts the objectivity of all SFG and tries to induce linguistic structure almost without reference to any linguistic theory, which is somewhat not penetrating and theory-wasting; the shortcoming of a corpus-based or grammar-driven approach is that the attestation of an theory is based on the correctness of another theory, in which, if the referential theory is not sound, the attestation of the other theory, of course, is not reasonably dependable. What is more, the way of heavily annotating clauses forms an obstacle for the scale of the corpus, which makes the linguistic data biased before a research begins. Seeking for a solution to the three contradictions above, we need a systemic and comprehensive penetration into the incorporation of CL or corpora into SFG. An experimental incorporation of CL/corpora into SFG has been tried out as in the following.

The essence of the contradictions between corpus-based and corpus-driven approaches is whether linguistic data are tagged or annotated in a corpus. A corpus-based approach supports linguistically-marked data, while the corpus-driven one not. As has been dealt with previously, this deep and detailed theory-based annotation seriously confines the scale of the corpus, which is the precondition of the objectivity of the corpus-helped research. Furthermore, if some aspect of the theory in SFG is not sound, the result of corpus research is, therefore, not convincing. Meanwhile, no tagging or the annotated corpus advocated by Sinclair is not what we mean to propose either because the pure induction from the retrieved lines from the corpus without any theory is sporadic and superficial.

What is proposed here is a corpus-supported approach, which is not corpus-driven, corpus-based or a mixture of both. Before making a detailed elaboration on the corpus-supported approach, we'd better start with the features of major basic components of this method. The most basic and imperative component in the approach is the process of linguistic data in the corpus and its attached processing features. A properly-processed corpus can make the concordance lines more linguistically informative, but not so linguistically heavy as to be pre-biased by the theory, which ensures the objectivity that is attained by finding linguistic facts or regularity with the least prejudiced observation under the whole detailed framework of this approach. In addition to that, more grammatical information should better be marked with less time and labor in a semi-automatic or automatic way.

What is the proper annotation in the corpus-supported SFG research? Let us first come to the conception of annotation, which is the process of marking the additional specific linguistic information on linguistic units in the corpus, especially marking at the syntactical level. There are three other similar names for the marking: encoding, tagging and markup. Encoding is a way of representing elements in texts such as paragraph breaks, utterance boundaries in a standardized way across a corpus, so that they can be more easily recognized by computer software and by corpus users (Baker, Hardie & McEnery 2006: 66-67). The first part of encoding is the meta-language markup that is usually a complete and scrutinized framework including the most basic information about a text in a corpus such as genre, author, date, title, e.g. Standard Generalised Markup Language (SGML), Text Encoding Initiative (TEI) and Codes for the Human Analysis of Transcripts (CHAT). The second part is the markup of lexical information, parts of speech and syntactical information at the lexico-grammatical level.

The proper annotation can ensure the large-scaled processing of the linguistic data in a corpus. The easy way of processing the large-scaled linguistic data is of the first importance because it is the precondition of the representativeness of a corpus. Representativeness is, in turn, prerequisite for the objectivity in a corpus-based or driven research. The functional variety in certain context or contextual configuration (situational context, social-culturally context and the relationship between both) and the representativeness are emphasized in SFG, and thus the representative corpus is the one that consists of enough texts of language varieties to catch the maximum representativeness in designing a corpus.

There are some methods of catching the representativeness. Random sampling techniques are standards of many areas of science and social science, and the same techniques are also used in building a corpus. Specifically, the method uses a comprehensive bibliographical index, through which the Lancaster-Oslo/Bergen (LOB) Corpus is constructed by the builders who use the British National Bibliography and Willing's Press Guide as their indices. Another approach is to define the frame of texts like all the various reading materials in a special library of a particular discipline, through which the Brown Corpus is built. Distinctive from the two methods above, Biber (2000) also points out the advantage of determining beforehand the hierarchical structure (or strata) of the population. This refers to defining the different genres or channels of which it is composed. Stratificational sampling is never less representative than the pure probabilistic sampling, but is often more representative, as it allows each individual stratum to be subjected to probabilistic sampling (Baker, Hardie & McEnery 2006: 139-140).

4.2.2 Proper Annotation and Its Theoretical Basis

The previous section identifies the corpus-supported SFG research with both the annotation and representativeness in sampling linguistic data to build a corpus, in which the annotation is the basis and prerequisite for the representativeness of a corpus. Therefore, the identification of the proper annotation is the key to understanding and defining the corpus-supported approach to SFG. The proper annotation of the corpus-supported SFG is a semi-automatic process that annotates clauses both lexically and grammatically. It begins with the KWIC[①] (key word in context) in CL and annotates clauses through formalizing and micro-modeling the linguistic features of the system and function in SFG in the form of certain patterns of lexico-grammar that can be retrieved. The automatic realization of annotation is that we can first

---

① KWIC is a concept in CL, and it refers to the key word in context. Key word is the node in a concordance that is a list of all the occurrences of a particular search term in a corpus. Context is the one in which key word is retrieved, and it contains a few words on the left and right of the key word.

automatically retrieve the SFG-featured items and annotate them all at once with the software designed under the fine theoretical framework of SFG. The core of automatic annotation is the formalization or further modeling of the theories in SFG into the lexico-grammatical patterns retrievable in concordance software or approachable in the way of CL. On the other hand, this method is also manual, which is mainly represented in two aspects: firstly, not all the items retrieved by the formalization of lexico-grammatical patterns comply with the required expectations, that is to say, there are some exceptions that must be checked out automatically; secondly, not all the theories or theoretical features can be formalized or micro-modeled into the lexico-grammar patterns that can be retrieved, and some are not retrievable, even though they can be realized in lexico-grammatical patterns.

Therefore, the annotation in the corpus-supported SFG is a semi-automatic way, of which the core is the formalization or micro-modeling of the theories and theoretical features into lexical patterns. This is a completely new tentative approach that must be penetrated in both theory and practice in order to keep this method sound and well-founded. The realization of the formalization or micro-modeling of theories and theoretical features into lexical patterns is actually a process finding the equation between form and meaning at a higher level. Linguistic or other modes of forms are the realization of meaning, but not all meanings can be realized in linguistic forms. So why and how the lexical patterns realize the equation between form and meaning are the first questions to answer to penetrate into the proper annotation in the corpus-supported SFG, of which the essence is the formalization or micro-modeling of the theories and theoretical features into lexical patterns or strings.

To realize the formalization or micro-modeling of the theories in an acceptable way in CL, we'd better find the nature of CL and its ideas of the process of linguistic data because it is the first stop from which we can go to our destination for the corpus-supported SFG research. Corpus-featured CL has existed for a period of time. Sinclair (1991: 115) defines CL as collecting naturally-occurring texts to study the features of language variety and model. Namely, CL is a texts-crossing study, which is expected to reveal more objective linguistic information than that from analysis of a single text (or analysis of several texts) if a texts-crossing way is properly annotated. How a corpus is annotated depends on the common ground of the nature of both the corpus and SFG. Togini-Bonelli (2001) believes the purpose of the corpus is to explain, attest, illustrate, or describe linguistic phenomena, while Yang (2002: 13) believes the goal of CL is to process the unlimited real linguistic data based on the research on real linguistic material. Tognini-Bonelli's definition is result-motivated, whose realization must depend on the applicability of processing the unlimited real linguistic data discussed by Yang. The main idea of Yang's process of the large-scaled data is not only the basis of the realization of Tognini-Bonelli's ideas about CL, but also the prerequisite for Baker's thoughts (2006: 49), which is mainly about the linguistic probability proof in linguistic study and probability information research based on the concordance and statistics of real linguistic data. It is asserted in SFG that linguistic system is a meaning choice potential, and the meaning construction through language is a probabilistic choice. The linguistic character of probability is the common ground to both SFG and CL, that is to say, both the linguistic disciplines are basic quantitative research to some extent based on the real linguistic proof and linguistic probability. Either the attestation of linguistic data or the description (including explanation) of linguistic phenomenon is basically quantitative. The first step of quantity research must be the quantitative study of linguistic forms, into which meaning, linguistic theories and their features are expected to be transformed. The transformation is not a simple process of transforming those into the lexico-grammatical patterns, but what is more, into the linguistic forms or patterns that can be retrieved or annotated automatically, which is the key to the quantitative linguistic study based on the automatic process of large-scaled corpora.

Let us move on to the transformation between theory and lexico-grammar in SFG. As is touched on above, the core of annotation is the formalization or micro-modeling of the theories and theoretical features into lexical patterns that can be retrieved and annotated automatically, which is the goal and essence of the corpus-supported SFG research. The applicability of this annotation should be explored before we move on. In both SFG and CL, language is considered as a social phenomenon, and language study is based on the natural language usage and naturally-occurring texts. In SFG, language is probabilistic in that it is a potential system of meaning choices, whose realization is the meaning construction through the choice of the network of lexico-grammar under certain context that determines the skew coverage of the probability of the network of choices from potential to realization. It provides the possibility of the annotation in the corpus-supported SFG research, and both the probability of language and linguistic meaning are represented as the probabilistic patterns of lexico-grammar in SFG. What is a lexical-pattern in CL? Concerning meaning and probabilistic choices of texts, Sinclair (1991: 109) proposes the open-choice principle, "This is a way of seeing language text as the result of a very large number of complex choices. At each point where a unit is completed (a word, phrase, or clause), a large range of choice opens up and the only restraint is grammaticalness". Sinclair's opinion on text is that it is the result of an open probabilistic choice from language system, which agrees with Halliday's ideas. Let us move further on to the realizing process of a text or the choice realization in lexico-grammar in CL. Sinclair (1991: 110) concludes the idiom principle as "…that a language user has available to him or her a large number of semi-preconstructed phrases that constitute choices, even though they might appear to be analyzable into segments. To some extent, this may reflect the recurrence of the similar situations in human affairs; it may illustrate a natural tendency to economy of effort; or it may be motivated in part by the experiences of real-time conversation". Sinclair emphasizes the phraseology in the corpus research for it is both the reflection on the human habitual linguistic behavior and the result of economy of effort. The units in phraseology are the semi-set expressions of lexico-grammar, which mediate between the set ones and the free ones, so we can derive that phraseology is a study on the cline between lexis and grammar.

Are the lexico-grammatical patterns in SFG and the ones in CL completely the same? No, they are not. The distinction between them can be concluded as follows: the lexico-grammatical patterns in SFG are paradigmatic while the phraseology in CL is syntagmatic; the lexico-grammatical patterns in SFG are a vertical probabilistic profile of the metafunctions, but the ones in CL are the horizontal collocation between or among specific lexical items quantified by Z-score; the former are the potential choice, or probabilistic choice while the latter are the result of choices; as for a specific text, the probabilistic choice is the realized form of the skewness of a probabilistic profile. The differences illustrate that the syntagmatic collocation is not contradictive with the paradigmatic probabilistic profile, and both of them are the language study of different phases on the successive processes of meaning construction. Construing meaning begins, not with the lexis, grammar or lexico-grammar, but with the probabilistic profile in SFG. It guides the meaning-construing process and provides the variants in the result of construing meaning, and thus the lexico-pattern in SFG is the feature in the construing process. The one in CL is the final stage and the result of meaning construction. Meaning is usage in CL but a linguistic construction in SFG, and both the features illustrate a relationship between result and process.

Therefore, both lexico-grammatical patterns in SFG and CL are, instead of contradictive, complementary, in which the result frequency findings are references to the probabilistic profile in the process of construing meaning. The complementarities are mutual in that the paradigmatic probabilistic profile guides and confines the horizontal patterns of collocates, which, in return, indicates the vertical probable patterns. As is discussed above, the corpus is lexis-preferable and concordance is actually lexical or lexical pattern-retrievable. The probabilistic profiling in the corpus-supported SFG research is expected to be established by observing the skew of the frequency pattern shown by the collocation of lexico-grammar in the texts of the same genre in the corpus. To make the complementarities more concrete and easily operable, both the representations of the probability profiling in SFG and the frequency pattern in CL are to be studied for more details. First, let us come to the potential choice system in SFG. Firth (1957) proposes the system concept, which is simply a kind of a colligation. Halliday (1966) develops the system and its related elaborations, all which constitute the systemic grammar, "A systemic grammar is a paradigmatic grammar in which the fundamental organizing concept is that of the system: that is, a set of options with a condition of entry, such that exactly one option must be chosen whenever the entry condition is satisfied. A system is thus a kind of 'deep paradigm'." Later on, discussions by Halliday (1976, 2004), Halliday and Martin (1981), Matthiessen (1988, 2002), Fawcett and Tucker (1990), Wu (2000) and Neale (2002) demonstrate such a similar view: linguistic system is a vast network of probabilities of choices of lexico-grammar, by the realization of which meaning is construed on an entry condition. This network consists of many micro-systems, which, in turn, contain more micro-systems. The linguistic system is a system network of lots of micro-systems, which are realized paradigmatically, that is to say, their realization is a paradigmatic choice. Therefore, it is concluded that the meaning construction is a process through which systems or micro-systems are instantiated into lexico-grammatical instances by paradigmatic choices, and the instantiation is the realization of the probability system as the form of lexico-grammar or instances.

The discussions above show that instances are the result of paradigmatic choices from the system, but the lexico-grammatical forms of instances (that is, the clauses) are syntagmatic, whose constituents are combined horizontally. The ultimate purpose of the corpus-supported approach to SFG research is to establish the paradigmatic probabilistic profiling from the concordance and statistics of the frequency of the syntagmatically-combined clausal constituents. The establishment of the inner vertical profiling from the outside horizontal combination requires a systemic and penetrative exploration. We have elaborated on the aspect in SFG, and now we move on to this topic in CL. CL focuses on collocation through retrieving KWIC with its statistics. What is the inner relationship between horizontal collocation and vertical probabilistic choice besides the one between process and result talked about above? Halliday (2004: 11) expresses his views on collocation and paradigm through a detailed discussion on co-hyponyms, the members of a thesaurus:

Another way of thinking about this shared (common) privilege of occurrence that unites the words in one paragraph of the thesaurus is in terms of **collocation.** Collocation is the tendency of words to keep company with each other: like *fork* goes with *knife, lend* goes with *money, theatre* goes with *play.* Of course, if words do regularly collocate in this way, we shall expect to find some semantic relationship among them; but this may be quite complex and indirect. Collocation is a purely lexical relationship; that is, it is an association between one word and another, irrespective of what they mean. It can be defined quantitatively as the degree to which the probability of a word y occurring is increased by the presence of another word x. If you meet *injure,* you may expect to find *pain* somewhere around: given the presence of the word *injure,* the probability of the word *pain* occurring becomes higher than that determined by its overall frequency in the English language as a whole. The words that are grouped into the same paragraph in a thesaurus are typically words that have a strong collocational bond: either with each other or, more powerfully, each of them with some third party, some common associate that forms a network with them all.

The relationship between or among the co-hyponyms of a thesaurus is defined as the semantic relevance in Teubert's view (2004: 93), "it is a unit of meaning in its own right, a collocation not just on the basis of the frequency of co-occurrence of its elements, but also on the basis of semantic relevance". It is concluded from the thoughts of both Halliday and Teubert that the frequency information of words in collocation is an indication of the probability of a word relative to its co-hyponyms in its thesaurus, and meaning comes out of the probabilistic choices and shows the semantic relevance instead of semantic meaning in collocation. What is more, it is theoretically correct to engage a penetration in the probabilistic profiling methods from the perspective of collocation. Let us move on to collocation to find its nature and value in profiling probability. Collocation is proposed in the 1930s by Palmer and Hornby in their *Second Interim Report on English Collocations* (1933), and later mainly by Firth (1957) in his "Modes of Meaning" and by Sinclair (1991), McEnery (1996),

Kennedy (1998), Biber, Conrad and Reppen (1998), Stubbs (2001), etc. Halliday et al. (2004: 168) define collocation and its profile as follows: collocation is "the habitual meaningful co-occurrence of two or more words (a node word and its collocate or collocates) in close proximity to each other; as a lexical relationship, collocation can be defined quantitatively as the degree to which the probability of a word y occurring in text is increased by the presence of another word x". And the collocation profile is "a computer-generated list of all the collocates of a node word in a corpus, usually listed in the order of their statistical significance of occurrence". The latest discussions by Halliday (2008: 37-38) are lexis-preferable as follows:

> The lexical set was defined by collocation: its boundaries were indeterminate, but the members of a set shared the same collocational environments (that is, the words with which they tended to co-occur were the same...Sinclair and I saw this (collocation) as a formal relation among lexical items that was manifested in quantitative terms. It was the extent to which the probability of a word is perturbed by the environment in which it is occurring: specifically, by the other words occurring around it, at least within a certain distance. The nature and extent of this distance remained to be empirically determined; our best guess was a span of four or five lexical words on either side of the node.

We have seen the crossroads between the vertical systemic probability and the horizontal instantiating collocation. The intersection is what we should focus on. What we try to figure out is a model through which the vertical probability profile can be established from the horizontal frequency of collocation.

4.2.3 Vertical Probability Profile Established from the Horizontal Frequency of Collocation

4.2.3.1 Mechanism of the Formalizing/Modeling Theory Through the Intersection of Collocation Frequency in CL and Probability Profile of Systemic Choices in SFG in the Corpus-Supported Application

The computational and quantitative study of collocation focuses on quantifying the relationship of a node (key word in context) with its collocates (the words within the span). A computational and quantitative approach to SFG is to figure out the probabilistic profiling of the linguistic potential system. Concerning the computational and quantitative studies in SFG, Webster (2005: vii) comments, "for Halliday, this has meant modeling language paradigmatically, contextually, functionally, fuzzily and developmentally". Therefore, establishing linguistic probabilistic profiling is multi-dimensional, comprehensive and specific. Probability is the inherent quality of the corpus-supported annotating model. Linguistic probability can be reflected on the instances in a corpus by the model. Gui's (2004: 3) ideas may be a reference, saying the domestic linguistics should adhere to the tradition of the linguistic data and probabilistic method, meanwhile, we'd better develop CL to establish the modern and ancient Chinese corpora to study the psychological cognitive models of Chinese processing. The model is the probabilistic one on linguistic choice and its realization. In the corpus-supported SFG research, the linguistic construing model should be probabilistically established, covering the crossing textual probability and clausal probability modes in metafunctions, which is, actually, derived from the lexico-grammatical realization patterns under a certain contextual configuration. However, the present study is mainly on the crossing-texts syntagmatic combining probability research, neglecting the starting point of the syntagmatic constitution, that is, the paradigmatic thesaurus choice probability from which meaning is originally built. The thesaurus choice is concerned with the word-class members for a potential choice in certain context. The lexico-grammar is represented as a vertical choice network, in which lexical choice is the completely vertical linear potentiality. The probability profile of a lexical linear potentiality can be constructed by retrieving the thesaurus of nodes established beforehand. The linear lexical concordances in a thesaurus are a kind of vertical co-occurring probability, namely, a comparative study on the contrastive features among the paradigmatic characteristics of all the co-hyponyms in a thesaurus. First of all, let us come to CL to see the applicability when applying this corpus approach to SFG research.

4.2.3.2 Representativeness of a Text and Crossing-texts Analysis in the Corpus-Supported Application

What is more concerned in the approach is how to reach, in corpus data, the representativeness that is the certification and assurance of the objectivity and comprehensiveness of the concordance result. This representativeness is mainly about the genres of some chosen texts and shows the distinctive features in many aspects of SFG and CL. In SFG, genre is the same as register, and both are replaceable (though Martin distinguishes them in his evaluation system for specific research purpose). Halliday (1964) argues that register is a functional variety of language. The functional variety of language is context-specific, in which context determines the characteristics of a discourse or texts. The contextual (including situational and socio-cultural) information is modeled and incorporated into the lexico-grammatical meaning construing, which forms the genre features of the text construed. The incorporation of situational information and modeling into lexico-grammatical texts is mainly concerned with the contextual configuration proposed by Halliday & Hasan (1976), who develops Gregory and Carroll's (1978) ideas of context theory of field, tenor and mode. Representativeness is expected to be related to many aspects, such as the proportion between academic and non-academic degrees related to field; formal or intimate ones to tenor; spoken or written ones to mode etc. More detailed classifications can be made in each above, like the academic one consisting of the highly academic style in academic articles and the less academic ones. Halliday (2004: 4-5) himself prefers a single text analysis to the crossing-texts one because he is particular about contextual influence on meaning analysis: "This in turn means recognizing that the contexts for analysis of discourse are numerous, and varied-educational, social, literary, political, legal, clinical and so on; and in all these the text may be being analysed as specimen or as artifact..." However, a single text analysis has its own limitations. The very imperative one is, to what extent the linguistic analytical result is representative and objective because one text does not represent most texts in the same genre or the similar context as the taste of one apple does not tell the flavors of all apples of all varieties in a lot of different places. As for text analysis in SFG, what is equally important to context is the approach of linguistics that must be coherent, comprehensive, and multi-dimensional. That approach of linguistics to texts in situation is called linguistic stylistics, "...It is the latter that may reasonably be called 'linguistic stylistics'...It is a prerequisite of such a study that both the theory and the description should be those used in the analysis of the language as a whole...this is the only way to ensure the theoretical validity of the statements made" (Halliday 2002b: 5). However, the coherent, comprehensive, and multi-dimensional approach of linguistics cannot ensure the representativeness in the analysis of a single text, which is just one sample of its genre. One outline of a mountain cannot tell or come more closely to all the main features of all mountains. The corpus-supported approach to SFG should be a crossing-texts analysis in which analytical results of more than one text are compared in order to conclude the valuable linguistic findings for both a single text and the genre in which it is a sample. That is the major way to reach the representativeness of linguistic data in the application of the corpus-supported approach to SFG.

4.2.3.3 *Specific Operational Methods in the Corpus-Supported Application*

While, instead of rejecting the analysis of a single text, the corpus-supported approach to SFG combines a single-text way and a crossing-texts one in a uniquely complementary way to make both the linguistic modes support each other with its advantages. Though the reasoning conclusion is less objective, the advantage that the analysis of a single text takes over the crossing-texts one is that the former is more penetrative and revealing because all the detailed syntactical annotation is manually made with more active and creative human participation. Halliday's analytical style by analyzing a single text with overall systemic grammar (1964, 1971, 1977, 1982, 1987, 1990, 1992, 1994) tells more about a specific text than the crossing-texts way whose annotating process is less actively and humanly involved. In one of Halliday's classical analysis articles, "Linguistic Function and Literary Style: An Inquiry into the Language of William Golding's *The Inheritors*" (1971), Halliday makes a penetrative and systemic analysis of the transitivity composition in great detail. Even in the analysis of a single text, only three segments of it are chosen to represent the whole of the analyzed text and texts of that period in history. Halliday (2002c: 108) refers to his way of analysis as: "For this purpose I shall look closely at three passages taken from different parts of the book; these are reproduced below (pp. 121-124). Passage A is representative of the first... Passage C is ... concerned with the tribe; while Passage B spans the transition, the shift of stand point occurring at the paragraph division within this passage." His finding is that the transitivity structures are different before and after the invasion by observing the transitive and voice aspects which are not used or less employed before being invaded, but increasingly appreciated with the temporary extension of invasion.

Though suspicious of the representativeness and objectivity of the linguistic findings of the article by Halliday, I firmly believe its great value to be much more revealing and enlightening for further linguistic research, attestation and modification to come closer to the truth. The approach of linguistics to a single text by the manual annotation suggests what is deeply hidden in a text. No one does better than Halliday with his way of linguistic stylistics. But my personal view is that the linguistic findings based on a single text or several texts show their value mainly in the linguistic prediction instead of guidance because we are not sure that one text or several texts can reveal the representative linguistic features of all texts in certain phase in history or in its genre. More revelations and enlightenments indicate the prediction of a linguistic discovery instead of guidance in its register.

We can conclude that a single-text-based (several-texts-based) analysis in linguistic stylistics is more predicting than regulating. The findings need to be further attested to judge whether the revelations are common or not by a crossing-texts approach. If the predictions from a single text way are attested existent across texts within a genre or a phase in history, the predictions guide linguistic findings; if not, the anticipations should be repaired, modified, complemented or even rejected if they are misleading. In contrast, the crossing-texts approach is more dependable because its result is founded on more representative concordances and more objective observation based on a large-scaled corpus. The approach plays a guiding role in many aspects of linguistic research besides a attesting one. In addition to retrieving what cannot be found in a single text, a crossing-texts approach provides a standard to judge the significance of the findings from a single text analysis, guide the direction of a single text analysis in return and make decision to dispose the findings, such as for further modification, correction, or abandonment.

However, a crossing-texts approach has its shortcomings and limitations compared with a single text one. Findings from the analytical results of a single text are sharper and more piercing and pioneering while the ones from the other way are more reserved and cruder, which deserve greater efforts to analyze for further more linguistic revealing information. The single text analysis is more intelligent while the crossing-texts analysis is more superficially formalized. Analysis of a single text reveals more original ideas while a crossing-texts one is less creative but more observational and reasoning. The method of the former is based on the characteristics of linguistic observation while the one of the latter is founded on the statistics of the regularities of the linguistic features retrieved from the corpus. The former is time-and-labor-saving while the latter is time-and-labor-consuming. Concerning the operational method, the former is much too simpler than the latter. It tells them apart whether the reasoning observation is on the linguistic data of segments of a single text (a single text and several texts of similar characteristics) or on a lot of texts chosen in a balanced way from a corpus. Despite the disparities between them, the common background shared by both methods is that both of them are based on the reasoning from the observation on the linguistic data that are the foundation of the true and objective conclusion.

In the corpus-supported approach, SFG serves as an analytical instrument in the genre (context)-specific text(s) with a combination of both analyses of a single text and a large number of texts. Before dealing with the concept for further detail, we'd better come to Halliday's concept of linguistic stylistics.

Webster (2002: 5-6) talks about the application of linguistics to the analysis of texts, besides, he confines the linguistics in the text analysis in his comments on Hallidayan linguistical approach to text analysis and textual meaning,

Linguistic stylistics must be an application, not an extension, of linguistics; this is the only way to ensure the theoretical validity of the statements made...At the same time the descriptive statements made about a literary text are meaningful only in relation to the total "pure" description of the language concerned: if the linguist hopes to contribute to the analysis of English literature he must first have made a comprehensive description of the English of the period at all levels. ... If for example all clauses of a particular poem are shown to have the same structure, it is essential to know whether or not this is the only permitted clause structure in the language; and if not, what its relative frequency is in a large sample representative of "the language in general".

Webster (2002: 6) continues to comment,

Linguistic stylistics is thus essentially a comparative study. To pursue the example above, we also need to know the relative frequency of this clause structure in other works of the same period and the same genre. The more texts are studied, the more anything said about any one text becomes interesting and relevant. We can therefore define linguistic stylistics as the description of literary texts, by methods derived from general linguistic theory, using the categories of the description of the language as a whole; and the comparison of each text with others, by the same and by different authors, in the same and in different genres.

Concluded from above, Hallidayan linguistic stylistics is different from other linguistic approaches to texts. Halliday focuses on the comparative study on the probabilistic profile of the linguistic features in the different parts of a text, texts in a genre, and texts in the same or different historic periods. He is reserved on the norms in text study, and his way is distinctive from the traditional foregrounding theories (Leech 1965) mainly dealing with prominence as a deviation from (negative prominence) or attainment of (positive prominence) norms (the set backgrounding regularities of a textual style). Hallidayan linguistic stylistics is probabilistic in nature, "we are probably rather sensitive to the relative frequency of different grammatical and lexical patterns, which is an aspect of 'meaning potential'; and our expectancies, as readers, are in part based on our awareness of the probabilities inherent in the language. This is what enables us to grasp the new probabilities of the text as local norm; our ability to perceive a statistical departure and restructure it as a norm is itself evidence of the essentially probabilistic nature of the language system" (Halliday 2002c: 102). This probabilistic view is mainly represented and applied in Hallidayan distinctive concept of prominence in the application of his linguistic stylistics, "I have used the term 'prominence' as a general name for the phenomenon of linguistic highlighting, whereby some feature of the language of a text stands out in some way...I hoped to avoid the assumption that a linguistic feature which is brought under attention will always be seen as a departure" (Halliday 2002c: 99). Later he gives a deeper elaboration on prominence from the perspective of construing meaning, "much of the meaning of a text resides in the sort of foregrounding that is achieved by this kind of environmentally motivated prominence, in which certain sets of options are favoured..., as a realization of particular elements in the social context" (Halliday 2002c: 62). The probabilistic profile of prominence is constructed out of the comparative research into the relative frequency of the linguistic features within a text or across texts. What is more, the establishment of the profile of probability from the choices or relative frequency of linguistic features is motivated to the whole meaning of the text(s) studied. The whole construction of prominence structure is set under the meaning-construing framework.

It is concluded that the text analysis in the corpus-supported approach to SFG is a combination of both analytical methods. Each exerts its distinctive and positive roles. The mutual complementarities of the two ways will make the corpus-supported SFG more piercing and dependable, producing more pioneering and reasonable conclusions. Specifically speaking, the former is more efficient in proposing some sharper, piercing and pioneering ideas within the analysis of a text or several texts, but its result is more suggestive and referential than guiding in the corpus-supported approach to SFG. The crossing-texts method, the latter, is to attest and modify the ideas proposed by the first means through retrieving and observing more representative and balanced linguistic data. In addition to the function of attestation and modification, the crossing-texts approach can also reveal and predict theoretical suppositions, and some vague ideas in brain can be made increasingly clear and concrete by the observation on the concordance lines from a corpus. The complementarities of the two methods constitute one of the most important parts in the corpus-supported approach to SFG. The realization of combining the strong points of both methods in the approach is in the observation on the retrieved lines and their attached statistics of the relative frequency of the linguistic features of texts in the corpus.

4.2.3.4 Interrelationships Between Micro-Prominence and Macro-Prominence in Text Analysis in the Corpus-Supported SFG

The Hallidayan concept of prominence is expected to be more deeply penetrated into and pushed forward to be more inclusive and explanatory. Firstly, it is to be proposed that, within the span of prominence, there should be minor variations according to the linguistic data and research methods. Those variations show distinctions between micro-prominence and macro-prominence, each of which shows its distinctive characteristics respectively.

Micro-prominence suggests setting up the prominence scheme of the more particular linguistic features with the micro or finer observation and reasoning within a text or segments of a text. The method in micro-prominence is microscopic in which it looks for, magnifies and checks the minute and tiny linguistic features with a more specific presupposed outline. The linguistic proof found in the way is specified and text-confined, and it is more acute and pioneering for the linguistic reasoning and anticipation. It is the microcosmic research that is sensitive and innovative, which shows the great value in revealing the linguistic findings. The significance of this approach is its experimental role in discovering some foreseeing ideas. The concrete operational method of micro-prominence is the comparative illustration of the frequency of both the prominent and non-prominent linguistic features. Only through the foregrounding distributions or distributional patterns can the revealing regularity of the potential meaning-construing choices be found or concluded. The fine and minute comparable study of the relative frequency profile between foregrounding and non-foregrounding linguistic features is confined within a specific text that is less objective and representative. The operational method can be further divided into two kinds according to the extent to which the research covers. One covers the whole passage, and, in the other a few segments of a passage are selected to delegate all. The former is more distribution-concerned with frequency while the latter is more comparative and contrastive between the different segments selected from the perspective of temporality and content. Both methods are purpose-motivated and coherent meaning-motivated. This motivation requires that the representativeness of the selected segments from a text be important because the deviation from it is to move away from the meaning-motivation of a text. The statistics is, to a large extent, simple and manual in both methods of the micro-prominence because linguistic features are fewer than the ones from more texts. Most texts are manually tagged or annotated in micro-prominence, and the manual one here is time-saving and convenient with very limited linguistic data. Therefore, the less previously-outlined research is variable in its process to reach findings. In the process, the brave and creative ideas are encouraged if proved or supported by the limited linguistic data of the chosen text (or several texts) or segments of a text. The findings appear more anticipating and foreseeing, but require further attestation with large-scaled linguistic data. The fewer and less representative the linguistic data, the less general and common the conclusion.

Macro-prominence overcomes the disadvantages of using fewer and less representative linguistic data with the crossing-texts method. In macro-prominence, it is expected to establish the framework of prominence of more general crossing-texts linguistic features with the macro or statistical observation and reasoning with the help of the corpus and the retrieving and annotating tools. The method in macro-prominence is telescopic, and it assembles, condenses and runs across the linguistic features with the less specified pre-existing outline. The linguistic proof found in the way is thus crossing-texts, and the macro approach is more attesting and general for linguistic reasoning and concluding. The macrocosmic research is more reserved and less human-manipulated, and it demonstrates great value in what exists commonly across the linguistic data of more texts instead of confined one or ones. The worth of this approach is its attesting and empiric role in discovering the regularity generally existing in language. The concrete operational method of macro-prominence is the comparative illustration of the frequency of the prominent linguistic features. Through the foregrounding distribution, the regularity of potential meaning-construing choices can be found or concluded. The comparable study on probability through frequency is crossing-texts. The operational method can be further divided into two submethods according to the extent to which linguistic research covers. One covers the whole corpus and the other selects a few texts from a corpus. The former is more distribution-concerned with frequency, while the latter is more comparative and contrastive and it deals with different texts selected from the perspective of temporality and genre. Both methods are research purpose/genre-motivated. This motivation requires that the representativeness of the selected texts from the corpus be important. If the chosen texts cannot represent the required factors of temporality and genre, it diverges from the expectation of the research as supposed. The statistics is, to a large extent, multi-leveled and automatic in both methods of macro-prominence because linguistic features are too many to be manually coped with. Most texts are automatically tagged or annotated in macro-prominence, which is time-saving and convenient with the help of retrieving and marking software. Therefore, this more specific previously-outlined research is stable in its process. In the process, the proof-based or proof-driven ideas are encouraged if they are proved, supported or suggested by the large-scaled linguistic data of the chosen texts or the whole corpus. The worth of findings is more proof-attesting and persuasively conclusive, but it requires more efforts in more reasoning and theorization. The more large-scaled and representative the linguistic data, the more general and common the conclusion.

The two elaborations above show that micro-prominence and macro-prominence are synergic and complementary. Micro-prominence is acute and pioneering in proposing suppositions and predictions, or finding new linguistic indications that can be further researched, modified, verified, supplemented and attested by macro-prominence. The corpus-supported research into SFG backs up both micro-prominence and macro-prominence, combines the functions of both methods to make them synergic and complementary to each other and makes them serve better to come to the true nature of language.

4.3 Attestable and Empirical Nature of A Corpus-Supported Approach to SFG

A corpus-supported approach to SFG is more a new perspective on language study than a method of linguistic research. Traditionally, most linguists follow a way of theorizing on one or several linguistic texts, and even on coined phenomena of language to draw a conclusion. It is very dangerous for linguistic researchers to be after that approach because we do not know whether a conclusion from reasoning on few real facts or coined linguistic facts is truly reasonably dependable or not. Few linguistic facts and conclusions based on them are not persuasive because there is not a large amount of linguistic data to prove whether the facts are common and the conclusion is really reasonable. The absolute dialectical thinking and logic reasoning on no fact or few facts are to make linguistics too abstract to be touched by the real linguistic data that are the origin on which most linguistic research is founded. This way produces a consequence, that is, most research is too highly abstract to be reachable by the real linguistic facts. Linguistics becomes something that has almost no relation with the everyday language we use.

The corpus-supported approach to SFG proposed in the study is empirical in its essence, which advocates observation on a large number of the real or naturally-occurring linguistic facts to find something common, regular and reasonably dependable. The orientation from the huge everyday and naturally-occurring linguistic facts to linguistic theorization and reasoning tells the corpus-supported approach to SFG apart from most studies in SFG. Firstly, the observation on linguistic facts is realized through concordance and certain methods of statistics, and the final stage of the observation is to put up the statistical profile that directly indicates the regularity of language. In general, the true and naturally-occurring linguistic facts are of first importance in the corpus-supported approach to SFG. The empirical character of the approach is represented as the quality and collection of linguistic data that are the basis for later research. To be specific, the initial step in the empirical approach is to ensure the true data must be properly collected and fully and comprehensively represent a linguistic phenomenon in certain situation. Secondly, the observation is expected to be as objective as possible, which resorts to, to a large extent, the observational and reasoning method. In the initial stage of setting up the model of the regularity of a linguistic phenomenon or theory, it is the quantitative method that plays the major role because it ensures the objectivity of the model for further reasoning and theorization. Once the linguistic statistical profile is established for a safe and sound theorization, deeper reasoning and observation are more in a qualitative way than in a quantitative one. The quantitative method allows for the space for the researchers' subjective experience to function in achieving certain discoveries or conclusions. To be brief, the subjective reasoning from the objective observation of a linguistic statistical profile is what has to be followed in the corpus-supported approach to SFG. Being empirical is the prerequisite for being attestable.

In addition, in the corpus-supported approach to SFG, it is believed that most theories and conclusions should be attestable, that is, they should be reached by naturally-occurring language and be proved right or wrong by linguistic data. The requirement of attestation in the corpus-supported approach to SFG orientates the SFG research in a distinctive perspective. Attesting approach will make the linguistic research be something as it should be. Nowadays, most studies in SFG are almost purely theorizing on theories, some of which are not attestable by the real linguistic data. Some studies based on a single text or several ones are not safe and sound because it is hard to say the very limited data can represent all similar texts. The attestable quality in the corpus-supported approach is to change the tendency and make linguistic research come back to the place where linguistics comes from. The linguistic research in SFG is expected to come down to the earth to describe language phenomena and discover linguistic regularity. Theorization is not something too abstract to be felt or touched by the real linguistic data. The attestation here means that a large number of representative and balanced facts are the standard to attest whether a theory is reasonable or not. Meanwhile, the attestation here does not go to extreme, and it still allows for the great space for logic reasoning on attestable basis.

The fact is that there is a great distance between linguistic theory and facts, e.g. we cannot find more complicated meaning and grammar in huge linguistic data. That is the most basic reason for the present research peculiarity, that is, more abstract theories with less persuasive linguistic facts. Therefore, the core to the realization of the corpus-supported approach to SFG is to make theories come closer to linguistic facts for attestation. That demands that meaning and grammar be figured out into certain form automatically/semi-automatically retrievable and annotatable in a large scaled corpus. As is reminded above, heavy annotation at the clausal level will bias the research before it starts. What is advocated in the corpus-supported approach to SFG is the proper annotation in which only some attestable meaning and grammatical information are marked automatically. The attestable meaning and grammar refer to those that are the basic meaning and grammatical units like the concepts of constituents of figures in the ideational metafunction. The way of annotation will make texts informative enough for linguistic research; meanwhile, it will not bias the texts like the corpus-based approach to SFG advocated by Matthiessen.

4.4 Summary

A corpus-supported approach to SFG is more a new perspective on language study than a method of linguistic research. In the approach, most theories and conclusions in research should be attestable and reachable by a naturally-occurring language. However, there is a great distance between linguistic theory and facts, and more complicated meaning and grammar cannot be found efficiently in the huge linguistic data. Considering the problem, a corpus-supported approach to SFG is proposed to make theory and language come closer. The corpus-supported approach is proposed with its attached theory and application model. Both the corpus-based and corpus-driven approaches are hard to move on because of their respective disadvantages in dealing with a large amount of linguistic data in the corpus and the fine complicated theories in SFG. The corpus-supported approach is a new way, and it comes closer to corpora than the corpus-based one and penetrates more into theories than the corpus-driven one. The corpus-supported approach combines both single-text (or analysis of several texts) and crossing-texts analytical methods, because the former is more efficient in proposing some sharper, more piercing and more pioneering ideas and the latter is to attest and modify the ideas proposed by the first. The first method is realized in setting up the micro-prominence scheme of the more particular linguistic features with the micro or finer observation and reasoning within a text or segments of a text. The method of micro-prominence is microscopic in that it looks for, magnifies and checks over the minute and tiny linguistic features with a more specific presupposed outline. Macro-prominence tries to establish the framework of prominence of the more general crossing-texts linguistic features with the macro or magnified observation and reasoning with the help of corpora and retrieving and annotating tools. Macro-prominence is telescopic and it assembles, condenses and runs across the linguistic features with the less specified pre-existing outline. The linguistic proof found in this way is thus crossing-texts, and the macro approach is more attesting and general for the linguistic reasoning and concluding.

Meanwhile, the proposal of the concept of the corpus-supported approach to SFG has its problems to be solved before it can be realized in linguistic research. The key to the realization of the approach is the annotation at the clausal level in a more efficient way than manual coding. In the corpus-supported approach, a proper semi-automatic or automatic annotation of the large-scaled linguistic data is proposed, which is the assurance of an objective and representative result of research. Furthermore, the core of the proper semi-automatic or automatic annotation of large-scaled linguistic corpora is to model the theories of SFG into the lexico-grammatical strings that can be retrieved and annotated semi-automatically/automatically.

Chapter Five

A Corpus-Supported Approach to Constituents and Their Patterns Within Figures

In Chapter Four, the core of the corpus-supported approach to SFG is to model the SFG theories into the lexical patterns or strings that can be retrieved and marked semi-automatically/automatically. Corpora are friendly to lexis, and lexical preference is the basic principle in CL. Whether the minor-prominence scheme within a text or several texts or the macro-prominence one across texts is targeted, the most basic meaning unit in the research is the clause, of which the most basic construing unit is constituent. Besides, construing a figure starts from the lexical choices from meaning potential. Lexical choices and choice patterns are key to learning more about figures and their meanings in deeper sense; therefore, the observation on lexical meaning and function in corpora is worth noticing.

5.1 Theoretical Modeling for Concordance of Constituents and Their Patterns Within Figures

Once one has established a corpus, one may take one of the several approaches to analyze it. Those approaches include 1) an 'informal' use in which one searches the corpus for examples that suit one's purposes and then reports those examples; 2) a systematic, exhaustive analysis of all the relevant examples in the data; 3) a systematic and exhaustive counting of the conflicting contrastive features of some aspects of the language (Fries 1940). The three approaches classify Fries' projects according to the way he uses his corpus. Fries adopts the third, that is, the quantitative approach to data, in most of his larger projects. The third approach to corpora involves counting systematically and exhaustively the contrastive features of some aspects of the language found in corpora. In other words, it emphasizes the paradigmatic relations in the analysis of the data. Counting contrastive features allows one to identify the patterns in the use or the development of language. Fries expresses his reasoning in a lengthy passage in *American English Grammar* (1940: 34) where he describes how he intends to analyze the letters that constitute his data.

Meanwhile, Section 4.2 focuses on the theoretical basis and the model of corpus-annotation from the character of corpora, especially the quality of lexical preference in CL. The incorporation of CL into SFG is, in essence, an attestable method based on the concordance and the analysis of the real linguistic data under the framework of SFG. In addition, it demonstrates such a view that the corpus annotation starts with the representation of the systemic potential choices of meaning and moves from the meaning construction to their following realization through the choices of figures and their constituents. The specific realization of the model of corpus annotation in the corpus-supported approach to SFG is to set up the probability profile of the crossing-figures constituents by the observation on the linear functional co-occurrences of the lexical potential systemic choices in construing figures, and the most basic method is to study the features of the vertical choice probability of systemic members and their functions through corpus concordance. The preference of probability profile is also fundamental to crossing-texts annotation. To be specific, it is an efficient automatic syntactic annotation in the theoretical framework of SFG by editing the annotating frames and defining lexical features of the constituents in figures with the help of some automatic retrieving and annotating software. A study of the lexical probability profile of the choices of lexical meaning potential system is the primary and initiating step for the annotation at the syntactical level.

What we are most concerned about is how to establish the probability profile of the choices of the lexical meaning potential system. Construing meaning begins with choosing constituents of figures from the meaning potential system and combining constitutes of figures in the instantiating process. Of course, the combination itself is a kind of a choice that involves more logical and logico-semantic relationship. Let us first come to the meaning potential system of constituents of figures. In SFG, the paradigmatic dimension of figures is of first importance because its realization forms the syntagmatic extension of figures. Meaning is construed in the vertical choice but realized in the horizontal combination.

The concordance span of KWIC in corpora covers the lexico-grammatical context with the node as the center, and the node can be a single word, a phrase, or a partial grammatical structure that is to be retrieved by regular expressions. The corpus-supported approach to SFG begins with the choice from the lexical meaning potential. The concrete application measurements run as follows: firstly, the thesaurus of the retrieved words is expected to be built because it is the potential system of a node; the relationship among the items or co-hyponyms in a thesaurus is vertical, each of which has set, to some extent, the choice probability and varying choice probability with context in construing meaning; secondly, retrieve each co-hyponym as a node in a chosen corpus; thirdly, choose some (if too many concordance lines) or all (if possible) concordance lines to analyze the functions of the nodes as constituents in each part or all of a clause; fourthly, collect systemically the functions of each node and compare all the functions of one node with another's; fifthly, observe the collection of systemic analyses of all the nodes or co-hyponyms to set up the probabilistic profile of the potential choice system by making the statistics of the comparative frequency distributions of all the nodes retrieved. In addition to the concordance, choosing a corpus is of the same importance. As for selecting a corpus, besides considering the representativeness of the linguistic data in it, one should see to the research purpose and try to look for a proper corpus, proportionally choose parts of a corpus or even set up a required collection of texts as a corpus. The measurements above demonstrate such an idea that the data-finding is corpus-abiding by, while data-preparing and analyzing are system- and function-guiding. That is to say, it is CL-directed, but its purpose is SFG-motivated. The corpus-supported approach to SFG is the method that overcomes the lack of linguistic data and less representation of the single text's research in SFG. In practice, the approach to the research on constituents of figures abides by the standards of both the functions a constituent plays in a clause and in the system of paradigmatic dimension, which is the basis for the choice probability of the co-hyponyms of a thesaurus. The retrieved form of a node should be a lemma[①] without variant forms for the comprehensive concordance of all variants of the node.

5.2 Application of Theoretical Modeling to Concordance of Constituents and Their Patterns Within Figures

The following practice is an illustration. We choose a thesaurus of five co-hyponyms, *ban, prohibit, forbid, enjoin* and *interdict,* and then choose two balanced corpora, LOB (Lancaster–Oslo/Bergen) and BROWN (Brown University Standard Corpus of Present-Day American English), to see the vertical functional co-occurring probabilistic pattern from the frequency profiles built from a comparative study on frequency mode of each node. The specific process is divided into two sections: the first section is the certification of the original possible forms as lemmas, that is to say, lemmatization of all the nodes into verbs, adjectives, nouns etc. or variants like *ed*-form or *ing*-form. Any possible form can be a lemma to be retrieved, which is the assurance of the comprehensive and inclusive coverage of all the meanings and usages; the second is to establish the statistical profile from the frequency modes of each node and thus try to conclude the potential systemic probabilistic proportional distribution.

---

① In lexicology, a lemma is the item which occurs at the beginning of a dictionary entry; more generally referred to as a headword. It is essentially an abstract representation, subsuming all the formal lexical variations which may apply: the verb walk, for example, subsumes walking, walks and walked (Crystal 2008: 273).

Table 5-1   Functional Retrieval Table Based on Lemmas

Item	Corpus	Frequency				
		Process (Predicator) Active/Passive	Epithet Adjunct (Infinitive)	Epithet A (Pre-participle)	Epithet B (Pas-participle)	Participant/ subject (Noun/Gerund)
ban	LOB	9(3/6)	2	2	0	9
	BROWN	2(0/2)	1	0	0	7
prohibit	LOB	5(4/1)	1	3	0	6
	BROWN	9(5/4)	2	3	0	9
forbid	LOB	21(3/18)	0	7	5	0
	BROWN	11(1/10)	1	2	0	0
enjoin	LOB	5(4/1)	2	0	0	0
	BROWN	5(1/4)	1	0	0	0
interdict	LOB	1(0/1)	0	0	0	0
	BROWN	0	0	0	0	0

Table 5-2   Functional Statistical Table

Item	Corpus	Process (Predicator) (Active/Passive)/%	Epithet Adjunct infinitive)/%	Epithet A (Pre-participle)/%	Epithet B (Pas-participle) /%	Thing (Noun/ Gerund)/%
ban	LOB	40.90 (33.33/66.67)	9.09	9.09	0	40.90
	BROWN	20.00 (0.00/100)	10.00	0	0	70.00
prohibit	LOB	33.33 (80.00/20.00)	6.67	20.00	0	40.00
	BROWN	39.13 (55.55/44.45)	8.69	13.04	0	39.13
forbid	LOB	63.63 (14.28/85.72)	0	21.21	15.15	0
	BROWN	78.57 (9.09/90.91)	7.14	14.28	0	0
enjoin	LOB	71.42 (80.00/20.00)	29.58	0	0	0
	BROWN	83.33 (20.00/80.00)	16.67	0	0	0
interdict	LOB	100.00 (0.00/100.00)	0	0	0	0
	BROWN	0	0	0	0	0

Observed from Tables 5-1 and 5-2, some features of each co-hyponym are as follows: (1) *ban* mostly functions as thing; most cases in concordance lines and the statistics in the tables show that *ban* functions as passive process and the active ones are rare. (2) *prohibit* and *prohibition* occur at a high frequency, and the 'thing' function is more frequent than the one of process; the usage of *prohibit* is, in most cases, active, and *prohibited*, usually appearing in the past participle form, mainly serves as modifier. (3) *forbid* has no noun and gerund usages, and the only function as process is mainly passive; its past participle form *forbidden* and present participle form *forbidding* function as modifiers in most cases. (4) The main function of *enjoin* is process, and the infinitive form *to enjoin* has a high proportion. (5) The word *interdict* is rarely used.

The result from the corpus-supported approach to SFG is different from what we traditionally know about those words, especially the function of *ban* as thing in usage appears as often as or even more often than the function of process. Traditional distinctions are made typical as follows in a Chinese dictionary: "forbid vt.禁止; prohibit vt.禁止, prohibition n.禁止; ban vt.禁止, 取缔; interdict vt.禁止; enjoin vt.禁止"; besides, one to three sampling sentences are given (Pan 2003: 189). This ordinary explanation is rather simple and crude; what is more, some definitions are even misleading. For instance, the statement on the usage of *ban* is not correct because the highly-used form of 'thing' function is even not mentioned.

This vertical linear comparative study on the co-occurring functions of nodes in the corpus-supported approach to SFG guides the specific lexical usage, which is a more genuine reflection of the natural linguistic usage. The domestic scholars base their studies of the collocation usage on corpora retrievals from the perspective of the traditional grammar. He (2004: 59) retrieves corpora and finds that wrong explanations of some basic words like *give, see, make, have* and *take* are put into some textbooks in China. The probability profile concluded from the frequency patterns of the co-hyponyms retrieved from the corpus illustrate the lexical usage convention that can only be attained through a large-scaled corpus. "After mastering fundamental grammar, learning a foreign language reaches the advanced phase. Whether language usage is genuine or not depends on collocation... the appearance of the large-scaled corpus provides the foundation of the objective quantitative analysis and makes the lexical collocation study more scientific and comprehensive." (Yang 2002: 27-28).

5.3 Summary

In the corpus-supported approach to SFG, finding the patterns of constituents within figures is the primary step for the establishment of the probability profile of the micro-prominence structure and the macro-prominence of figures. It is realized by observing the linear functional co-occurrences of the lexical potential systemic choices in construing figures. Specifically, it is to study the features of the vertical choice probability of the systemic members and their functions through observing and reasoning on the retrieved lines from the corpus. In addition, the study of the lexical probability profile of the choices of the lexical meaning potential system is the primary and initiating step for the annotation at the syntactical level. In the corpus-supported approach to SFG, the vertical linear comparative study on the co-occurring functions of nodes retrieved shows the regularity in construing figures and guides, in return, the specific lexical usage. The establishment of the lexical choice probability profile and the construction of the functional model of a quantified probability of the usage of linguistic units are the basis and the pre-condition of dealing with the probability skewness of the constituents of clauses, crossing-clauses text, and crossing-texts stylistics.

Chapter Six

A Corpus-Supported Approach to the Ideational Metafunction

The feature of the representing mode in the corpus-supported approach is the lexicalization of certain theories or certain aspects of theories in the lexico-grammar into a lexical string or regex (regular expression) that can be retrieved and then annotated automatically. The mode of the corresponding implementation is the application of retrieved results from the corpus to inspire the linguistic research and attestation in SFG.

6.1 Theoretical Modeling for Annotating the Ideational Metafunction of Constituents

The primary task of the corpus-supported approach to SFG is to put the question to be researched into under the framework of SFG, therefore, constituents should follow addressing the syntactical concepts of SFG. Meanwhile, the corpus mainly serves as the means for attestation, extension, and penetration. As for the syntactical annotation of constituents, we have mentioned Nesbitt & Plum (1988), Biber (2000), Wu (2000), O'Donnell (2002), Halliday (2002a, 2008) and Matthiessen (2006), and they all believe that the large-scaled syntactical annotation is manual at least at present. Matthiessen (2010: 141) holds the idea that there is an inverse relationship suggesting that the more significant a system is in the organization of the lexico-grammar of a language, the harder it is to automate the process of linguistic data. Matthiessen's viewpoint is accepted by Halliday (2008), and Wu and Matthiessen have done manual annotation. We have talked about the disadvantages of manual annotation in the previous part in the corpus-based approach to SFG.

In the thesis, a different approach is tentatively proposed and targeted to annotate part of the linguistic information under the framework of SFG in the constituents of clauses in a semi-automatic and eventually automatic way. The automatic linguistic data processing is a necessary stage for the true realization of the corpus-supported approach to SFG. This semi-automatic/automatic approach moves its way deeper into the regularity of lexis of the corpus to seek for the revelations for the corpus linguistic data processing in the approach, because all automatic corpus data-processing software tools in CL are developed and designed based on the character of the corpus—lexical preference. All the efforts to automate the syntactical annotation at the clausal level in the complex grammar framework in SFG prove to be a failure with a lot of limitations introduced in previous chapters. Moving towards the automatic/semi-automatic syntactic annotation in the corpus-supported approach to SFG starts with considering the inherent quality of linguistic data, to which CL may come closer because CL has its more advanced automatic tools to process linguistic data.

Automatic software tools for processing linguistic data in CL have successfully reached high accuracy, and the tools are widely used in both CL and NLP, like taggers (CLAWS[1], Tree Tagger[2], SemanTag[3] etc.) and parsers (Stanford POS, ENGCG[4], PC-PATR[5], Penn TreeBank[6], Wag parser[7] etc.) Before we move to the mechanism of tagging or parsing, we'd better know two basic pairs of concepts: tag and tagger; parse and parser. Tag is an action to mark automatically the additional linguistic information on linguistic data in the corpus, and the tagging components consist of a system of codes that are the names of markers containing linguistic information. Code system is the

---

[1] CLAWS is an automatic POS tagging system developed by UCREL (Unit for Computer Research on the English Language). It consists of five separate stages applied successively to a text to be tagged— pre-editing, candidate tag assignment, multi-word unit tagging, tag disambiguation and post-editing. Tagging in CLAWS is highly accurate, with a consistent accuracy of 96%—97% in tagging c. 100 million words of the British National Corpus (BNC) (see http://www. comp.lancs.ac.uk/computing/ research/ ucrel/claws/).

[2] Tree Tagger is a language independent part-of-speech tagger developed within the TC project at the Institute for Computational Linguistics of the University of Stuttgart (see http://www.ims.uni-stuttgart. de/projekte/corplex/DecisionTreeTagger.html). It has been successfully used for tagging German, English, French and Italian texts, and can be adapted to other languages as well.

[3] SemanTag is a semantic tagger developed by Cooke. It generates annotation of progressively richer semantic representation right from a raw text. Each word of the final annotated text contains tags indicating its part of speech, word sense, and role within the sentence, and this information will then be used to construct matrices of semantic identifiers by using a word sense database like WordNet. One typical feature of the SemanTag system is the use of an API for its taggers and data resources, which enables others to build applications that use the semantic information produced by SemanTag.

[4] English Constraint Grammar (ENGCG) is a surface-syntactic parser of English developed by Voutilainen, Heikkilä & Anttila within the Constraint Grammar framework. It consists of two components: a morphological analyser and a reductionistic parser. Using a morphological description and a large lexicon, the analyser applies all conventional analyses to each recognized word; the parser then eliminates all illegitimate alternatives and retains an unambiguous correct one.

[5] PC-PATR is a syntactic parser originally developed by Stuart Shieber at Stanford University in the early 1980s (e.g. Shieber, 1984). It is a left corner chart parser, doing the parsing from bottom-up with top-down filtering based on the categories, and in a left-to-right order.

[6] Penn TreeBank is one of the largest and most influential parsing projects. Penn Treebank is a 4.8-million-word collection of texts tagged for word class and partially parsed to give labeled bracketed structures (Kennedy, 1998).

[7] Wag parser is a systemic parser initially developed by O'Donnell (1994) as part of the Electronic Discourse Analyser (EDA) project funded by Fujitsu, Japan. It reads in paragraphs of text, and produces a micro-semantic analysis of each sentence.

collection of markers, such as tagset NN, NP etc. in *CLAWS* code system. Tagger is a piece of software to tag or mark linguistic information on linguistic data in the corpus, and both tag and tagger are dealing with the lexical level, that is, coping with part of speech.

Parsing is the process to mark the linguistic data in the corpus with the syntactical information, adding automatically more linguistic information than tagging does to linguistic data at the clausal level. Parser is a software tool to parse clauses in the corpus automatically, such as *Stanford POS*. Parsing codes are usually the markers to suggest the syntactical meaning and function of constituents in clauses. The naming of markers is linguistic school-specific. For example, the way of corpus-based SFG names markers after the concepts and definitions in SFG, while most CL names markers after the traditional grammar, e.g. the markers or codes in *SysFan* by Matthiessen, *Coder* by O'Donnell, and *POS* by Stanford University are distinctive. There are still three more concepts to be made clear before we can move further on, and they are annotation, encoding and markup, all of which are more comprehensive, containing tagging, parsing and annotation and including adding meta-information to text such as author, date, genre, context etc. (for more information, please refer to the website: http: //vl-eee.fgk.uni-sb.de/registry/draft.html).

The corpus is established with texts or discourses, but it is lexical concordance-based. Lexical retrieval is the keynote of CL and the basis for processing linguistic data. All the software tools listed above process the linguistic data according to the lexical preference, which is characteristic of the nature of linguistic data. The lexical character of the corpus is the foundation for the automatic processing of linguistic data. Yallop (2004: 23) comments on the lexical role in the corpus: "...vocabulary can be seen as part of lexicogrammar, a lexicogrammar that represents the choices which users of a language make, a lexicogrammar that represents our ability to mean. For, ultimately, language is about meaning. The main function of language—and hence of words used in language—is to mean". The lexis-orientated way is supported by Halliday, who (2004a: 16) senses the role of lexical preference for processing linguistic data and summarizes its function in the corpora of OED (Oxford English Dictionary),

Collins COBUILD, BNC (British National Corpus), ICE (International Corpus of English), Bank of English, etc. as follows:

Towards the end of the twentieth century significant changes were taking place in the theory and practice of lexicology, largely brought about by the new technology available for data-processing and text-based research. The two critical resources here are the computer and the corpus. Existing lexicographical techniques have of course been computerized…Grammar was described by tabulating the various forms a word could take (as paradigms, e.g. the cases of a noun or the tenses of a verb) and then stating how these forms were arranged in sentences (as constructions, or structures in modern terminology). But vocabulary and grammar are not two separate components of a language. Let us borrow the everyday term wording, which includes both vocabulary and grammar in a single unified concept. What is important is to gain an overall perspective on lexico-grammar as a unified field—a continuum between two poles requiring different but complementary strategies for researching and describing the facts.

The citation above shows that Halliday confirms the lexical preference of the corpus and its role in automatic linguistic data processing. Later, Halliday (2005: 17) points out that the computerized linguistic data, that is, the automatic lexis-based annotation, have made great achievements in many aspects as is indicated in the following words, "By the 1990s lexicographers could draw on massive resources such as the British National Corpus, the International Corpus of English, and the 'Bank of English'… and indefinitely large quantities of text, from newspapers to transcripts of enquiries and parliamentary proceedings, began to be accessible in machine-readable form". At the same time, it can be reasoned that Halliday's thought on the unity of lexis and grammar proves that the lexical retrieval and annotation are also grammatical near the lexical end of lexico-grammar. Wording is the ordinary word used to show the mediation between the two poles of the unitary lexico-grammar, and the two ends are complementary and mutually suggestive, but not replaceable.

Almost all the annotating software tools are lexis-based, but they show the great limitations at the syntactical marking level because they try to reach the grammatical pole through the lexical one, to which there is a long distance not abridged. Lexis and grammar show a relationship of cline and complementation. They are different in nature and require the distinctive dealing schemes respectively. The present automatic annotating tools are inefficient in marking clauses at the fine syntactical level, while the tentative way from the grammatical pole by both Matthiessen with his *SysFan* and O'Donnell with his *Coder* proves not to be a success because their manual annotation is time-consuming and labor-intensive. The lexical preference improves the automatic annotation level, but the approach is hard to reach the pole of grammar. In addition, abiding by the grammatical annotation from the perspective of grammar pole gives a more detailed syntactical description, but it fails automating the annotation. The contradiction is acute and hard for the approaches from both poles to make concessions. Is there a compromise that not only ensures the efficiency of automatic processing of linguistic data but also realizes the minute grammatical, specifically, syntactical annotation? My answer is "yes" on condition that some suggestions be proposed as follows.

1) The lexical preference should be obeyed, which is the assurance of automatic linguistic data-processing. Without automatic data processing, the corpus-supported (even the corpus-based or driven) approach to SFG is impossible. If there is no automation in annotation and retrieval, the corpus marked with linguistic information cannot be set up since the manual annotation from the grammar pole is too time-consuming and labor-intensive to be realized. There is no manually annotated corpus that has been built up till now according to SFG, and the fact proves that it is not right to annotate from the grammar pole. Matthiessen does not name his parsed linguistic data as a corpus because it consists of only 6,500 clauses, for which he gives a name *archives*.

2) Grammar should not be ignored. The present set-up corpora meet the need for data resource and proof in SFG research, but the advanced automatic retrieval and annotation show less value in SFG research since both of them

contain less information at the grammatical level, especially at the clausal level. No automatic tools of retrieval and annotation attached to the large-scaled corpora set up till now are developed to show the detailed syntactical description, not mentioning that of the SFG syntactical information. On the one hand, there are rich linguistic data in all kinds of large-scaled corpora attached with advanced parsing and retrieval software tools; on the other, the researchers on SFG do not know how to exploit these resources to the full extent, or apply them to the research in SFG. The solution to the problem is that the grammatical information under the framework of SFG should be inserted into the lexical retrieval and annotation in processing linguistic data in CL.

3) What is most concerned and imperative is to find out how the linguistic information in SFG is incorporated into automatic lexical retrieval and syntactical annotation based on lexical preference. Without the way to realize automation in processing corpus data, the exploitation of corpora is harder and less efficient to deal with; without linguistic data in corpora being more grammatically-marked in the automatic way, the application of corpora to SFG is less meaningful. The only way to abridge the automatic retrieval and annotation at the lexical level and the grammatical level is to incorporate more grammatical information that needs the manual retrieval and annotation into the way in which the lexical automatic data processing is realized. To be brief and concrete, it is a process of lexicalizing the syntactical grammar in SFG into certain retrievable patterns or strings.

4) Most research-targeted grammatical information, but not all in SFG, is expected to be automatically retrieved and annotated in CL. It is too demanding to be necessary to incorporate all the grammatical information of SFG into the automatic concordance and parsing, but some research-targeted automation is proposed to be tentatively attained through the proper incorporation. The corpus-supported SFG depends on the application of the corpus as a research means. The automatic process of linguistic data ensures the possibility and the efficiency of this method, which consists of the automatic retrieving and the automatic parsing at both the lexical and grammatical poles. To realize the automatic grammar concordance, a proper regex system, which represents the grammar

through the lexical pole, is expected to be made to realize grammar as the lexical patterns that can be automatically retrieved. Automating the annotation at the syntactical level under the framework of SFG also resorts to the present automatic parsing tools, and the incorporation of part of SFG information into automatic parsing requires a previous process of the parsing scheme in which codes and their structure may be changed for the specific linguistic information in SFG.

In the following sections, I will elaborate on the supposed outline guided by the four proposals above. Both CL and SFG see meaning as the core of their branches. Meaning construction starts from lexis, and thus lexical meaning in meaning construction is not to be ignored. Li's (2010: 37) idea is that CL studies the meaning of a text from the meaning unit, which is the lexical item of certain structural pattern. The meaning unit can be paraphrased in reference to the co-occurring context of the same or similar meaning unit. The meaning unit in CL is a word or word pattern explained in more than its own context, that is to say, it is described by all the contexts of the same, even similar nodes across concordance lines. Though meaning representation is lexical or phrasal, the meaning unit is something that exists out of the concordance lines specified, in which meaning is begun to be discussed in CL. It is similar to the constituent in a figure in construing meaning in SFG since each constituent is a somewhat semantically and functionally independent unit in its role to contribute to the whole meaning of a figure. It is described in the definition of the lexical meaning unit in CL that it is possible and applicable to annotate more grammatical information into it because the lexical meaning unit itself is certain kind of grammatical combination or pattern, whose space can be further expanded to allow for more grammatical information to be added.

Aijmer (2008: 4) refers to four methods to retrieve texts because research data are a good reference to the incorporation of grammar into lexical patterns. The first one is one-to-one searching, a completely lexical concordance which involves investigating a linguistic form through a search term that only yields relevant hits. To use more technical vocabulary, precision and recall are both at 100%. The ease of capturing relevant examples, however, does not necessarily mean that no more work remains for the researchers, who will often go on to examine different discourse functions or semantic distinctions of the searched terms in question. So lexis is easy to be operated, but it shows less linguistic information. The second search method can be called *sampling* (Ädel 2003). It begins the incorporation for the first time. It involves the use of one or more search terms that are good examples of the linguistic phenomenon in question. Though the drawback is that not all instances of the phenomenon can be retrieved, the advantage is that the search terms used tend to yield a high number of relevant hits. When using this method, the researcher cannot claim to have covered all basis or to have mapped out a linguistic function in its entirety. Meanwhile, many valuable insights can still be provided, especially if the search term is a good indicator of the phenomenon under study. The indicating retrieval is not accurate and the retrieved data need to be sifted. For that purpose, we move to the third one. The third search method can be called *sifting* (Ädel 2003). Once the initial hits have been retrieved, they need to be sifted through, and a certain proportion will be manually discarded. Using the method, a researcher often needs to put a great deal of time into checking the retrieved data (before the actual analysis can begin). The advantage of this method tends to be that, once the sifting has been done, the remaining set covers all or most of the potential forms of the linguistic phenomenon one is looking for. Leaking and negligence cannot be avoided if the second and the third methods are used because the indicating concordance plus manual sifting is not so safe. The fourth method may overcome that problem. The fourth method can be called *frequency-based listing*. It involves the use of a frequency list (of individual words or collocations), specifically based on the corpus under investigation, as a starting point. Using such a list, a researcher goes on to select the relevant search terms that occur with high frequency. In this way, the search terms will be tailor-made for the corpus and the particular discourse studied. It is an effective way of using the corpus-assisted methods to spot the persistent patterns in a specific dataset.

Those four methods are, in essence, lexis-preferring, but become more and more lexical-patterned as more linguistic features are expected to be retrieved from texts. That increasingly grammaticalized tendency towards a lexical pattern can concordance more linguistic information. The more grammaticalized the concordance is, the more inaccurate the retrieved items are. That inaccuracy can be improved by sifting the retrieved results manually. The corpus-supported approach to SFG tries to find an automatic/semi-automatic method to retrieve and annotate corpora. The key to the method is to edit the regular expression that reflects the potential grammatical structure.

Here the regular expression is more extended than the traditional one here. The regex is defined as a type of strings that may include special characters, called wild cards[①], which mean the regular expression as a whole will match with more than one string. For instance, the full stop as a special character in a regular expression can represent any single letter. Regular expressions, sometimes known as patterns, are often used when searching a corpus. It is often easier to define a regular expression that matches the set of words in a search, than to search for each word individually and combine the results in the traditional way. For example, for an investigation into compound words of which the second element is house (for instance, greenhouse, hothouse), a search could be made for *house. The precise rules of what the special characters in regular expressions are and how they work may vary in different tools (Baker, Hardie & McEnery 2006: 138). A regular expression is usually shortened as a regex, and it has two distinctive parts: the first is the constant part, that is, the normal one that is for literal retrieval; the other part is the special codes that can concordance a collection of combinations of letters or digits that agree with the characteristics a code represents. Stubblebine (2007: 5) defines a regex as follows: a regular expression is a string containing a combination of normal characters and special meta-characters or meta-sequences. The normal characters match themselves.

---

① A wild card is a character that can stand for any other character in a regular expression. Wild cards allow more sophisticated searches in corpora to be carried out. For example, a concordance program could specify that the *character acted as a wild card, standing for a string of any characters of any length. It would be possible to search for any word that begins with the word *look* (for example *looked, looking, looker*) by carrying out a search on the string *look**. Other types of wild cards can represent any single character—the full stop character can often function this way in searching syntax, for example h.t will find *hat, hit, hot* and *hut*. Different concordance tools may use different (or no) wildcards in their search facilities (Baker, Hardie & McEnery 2006: 168).

Meta-characters and meta-sequences are the characters or sequences of the characters that represent ideas such as quantity, locations, or types of characters.

The regex above is concerned mainly with the limited lexical combination that retrieves the very simple structurally-featured lexical set of a required form. It is very inefficient in retrieval from the pole of grammar. The recent advanced corpora and their retrieving software support both plain texts and annotated ones in corpora, and thus the regex can be extended by the combination of both the regex meta-characters and the specific tagging set. The concordance in the corpus-supported approach to SFG is preceded by modeling the grammar in SFG into the retrievable matching pattern realized as the regex plus tagging set for retrieval. The ultimate goal of the corpus-supported approach to SFG should find its way into the probability of the choices in construing figures through the lexical constituents that can be processed in the syntactical concordance and annotation. The specific operations are in the following:

1) Set the concrete content of certain level of research, such as one of the three metafunctions.

2) Specify the research question and formalize the study question into certain structure, logical form or structural pattern, which is tried to be edited into a regex. The key to the transformation is that the necessary linguistic features should be fully represented in the patterned string and the ultimate transformed regex.

3) Concordance according to the regex edited from the formalization of the linguistic features characteristic of the research question, and find a proper concordance tool that supports the edited regex.

4) Sift the concordanced lines manually, checking whether all the retrieved lines are the required ones, and tick off those that do not fully agree with what the regex requires. There is a need for manual sifting because the regex is a formalized retrieval, while what we try to analyze is from the perspective of meaning.

5) Collectively annotate those that represent certain linguistic feature(s) with the marking names from the framework of SFG.

6) Set or design statistical items according to the research purpose after

attaining retrieval and annotation.

6.2 Annotating the Ideational Metafunction in the Constituents of Clauses from the Perspective of the Automatic Process

The six guidelines above show that concordance exists before annotation, which is opposite to the traditional way. Before moving to the specific measures of this approach, we'd better introduce the software tools necessary for the process.

The first one is *Wordsmith* developed by Scott and issued by Oxford University Press in 1996. The new editions with more functions have been publicized in recent years, while the major functions have not been changed. It is an integrated suite of programs for observing how words behave or are used in texts and corpora. Its main functions are concordance[1], the keywords list[2], and the wordlist[3]. Both plain and tagged texts are applicable (for more information concerned, please see www.lexically.net/*wordsmith*.).

UAM CorpusTool is a software tool specially developed for the SFG research. It is mainly for retrieving and annotating texts or corpora, and the marking framework and tagging set are SFG-orientated. Specifically, its annotating characteristics are as follows:

1) annotation schemes can be altered and even designed according to the research purpose;

2) concordance and annotation of each text are multiple leveled (e.g., NP, Clause, Sentence, whole document);

---

[1] It refers to any word or phrase as a node in context and the collocates or company a node keeps, including calculating retrieved items.

[2] It locates and identifies key words in a given text by comparing the words in the text with a reference set of words usually taken from a large corpus of text. Any word found to be outstanding in its frequency in the text is considered "key".

[3] It is a list of all the words or word-clusters in a text, set out in an alphabetical or frequency order.

3) the regex is across levels and the statistics are across subsets.

(For more details, please see: http://www.isfla.org/Systemics/Software/ Coders.html)

UAM CorpusTool is, like other SFG-orientated software, e.g. *SysFan*, a manual annotating one, but its advantages are easy operation and multifunctions (concordance, annotation and statistics). Concordance is more informative in that POS[①] and other marking sets and schemas are set in and the regex in concordance can be extended in multi-levels to retrieve the more complex grammatical information. Then more detailed linguistic specifications can be automatically retrieved. What is more attracting with the software is that the retrieved items can be coded or annotated collectively immediately.

In the corpus-supported approach to SFG, the advantages of *Wordsmith* and *UAM CorpusTool* are combined to try to realize the meaning retrieval through the formalized concordance. The complete meaning retrieval in the corpus is not realized by itself, and meaning is expected to be transformed into the formalized patterns represented by regexes to be realized by the lexical-grammaticalized nodes and context (concordance lines). The original idea of the meaning concordance is the construction of the thesaurus that needs explaining in a broader sense. The concept of a thesaurus is here defined as a collection of the grammatical units related to each other in the meaning perspective of SFG. According to the definition above, it is derived that the transitivity thesaurus contains the thesaurus of material process predicates. The material transitivity is classified by Halliday as follows:

Thesaurus of the material creative general intransitive process predicates:

appear, emerge, occur, happen, take place, develop, form, grow, produce...

Thesaurus of the material creative specific transitive process

---

① It is a piece of software applied in *UAM CorpusTool* to annotate part of speech at the syntactical level under a set marking framework.

predicates:

assemble, build, construct; compose, design, draft, draw, forge, paint, sketch, write; bake, brew, cook; knit, sew, weave; dig, drill; found; establish; open, set up...

The concrete steps of establishing a corpus are taken as follows:

1) tag all texts or the corpus with CLAWS;

2) retrieve the predicate verbs with Concordance Tool;

3) make a list of words of the retrieved predicate verbs with Wordlist Tool of *Wordsmith*;

4) establish the thesaurus of the researched aspect of SFG from the word list of a text or the corpus;

5) set and design the retrieving program and the set thesaurus into the retrieving wild card(s) or more inclusive regex;

6) put the texts or the corpus into the *UAM CorpusTool*;

7) readjust or design an annotating scheme according to the research and the framework of SFG;

8) put in the scheme;

9) retrieve first by the regex edited for the required data in the research;

10) sift the concordance lines manually to tick off and delete all that does not agree with the regex at the meaning level, and if necessary, add some more changes to the annotating scheme, the thesaurus, or the regex when considering some exceptions are valuable;

11) annotate all the checked concordance nodes automatically with the concepts in the annotating scheme.

In the following, a long tale named *The Little Lame Prince* (number of words: 46312; number of clauses: 2021) is taken as an example to illustrate the semi-automatic annotation of the transitivity in the ideational metafunction. At first, Wordlist Tool in *Wordsmith* is used to give a wordlist of the all words in *The Little Lame Prince* for annotation as follows:

WordSmith Tools — 2010-4-7 20:33:12

N	Word	Freq.	%	N	Word	Freq.	%
1	the	2,259	4.90	2	and	1,670	3.62
3	to	1,265	2.74	4	he	1,133	2.46
5	a	1,120	2.43	6	of	928	2.01
7	his	818	1.77	8	it	707	1.53
9	was	703	1.52	10	in	630	1.37
11	I	548	1.19	12	that	499	1.08
13	had	458	0.99	14	him	452	0.98
15	she	433	0.94	16	as	425	0.92
17	her	420	0.91	18	you	382	0.83
19	but	379	0.82	20	not	357	0.77
21	for	355	0.77	22	with	355	0.77
23	all	302	0.65	24	so	292	0.63
25	prince	289	0.63	26	be	256	0.55
27	at	247	0.54	28	little	238	0.52
29	have	234	0.51	30	which	216	0.47
31	said	197	0.43	32	is	195	0.42
33	on	188	0.41	34	what	188	0.41
35	they	187	0.41	36	when	177	0.38
37	or	168	0.36	38	if	166	0.36
39	this	163	0.35	40	very	160	0.35
41	who	159	0.34	42	me	157	0.34
43	there	157	0.34	44	would	155	0.34
45	one	151	0.33	46	no	149	0.32
47	them	147	0.32	48	like	144	0.31
49	my	144	0.31	50	by	143	0.31

……

Next, Concordance Tool in *Wordsmith* is started to retrieve the predicate verbs of the tale, and the following classification of the retrieved words can be automatic according to the pre-designed the thesaurus or some other devices such as *ed; be/am/is/are/was/were; would/will/could/can/might/may/should/ shall. After finishing the process, *The Little Lame Prince* is introduced into *UAM CorpusTool* and retrieved according to the pre-set or designed scheme the regex and the thesaurus within the coverage of the wild cards. For instance, the wild card representing material process contains the thesaurus of *did, happen, got, wave, grow* etc.; mental, *desire, choose, like, rejoice, thought, know* etc. The following step is to define the features and make *UAM CorpusTool* recognize those features and retrieve them. If necessary, some complementation is expected to modify the pre-supposed preparations. What is followed is to edit the regexes, such as the regex of material transitivity is edited like *select material if the little lame prince: clauses containing immediately '@doing verb'*; the mental one, *select material if the little lame prince: clauses containing immediately '@ mental verb'* (@referring to a class).

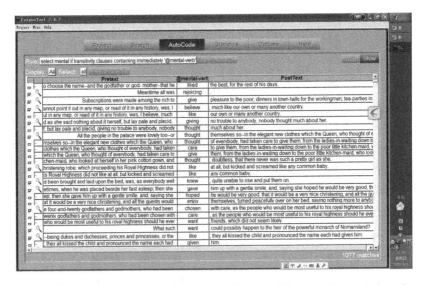

Figure 6-1   A Screen Shot of the Automatic Concordance and Annotation of Mental Process Transitivity

Then tick off and delete those exceptional or disagreed concordance lines with the manual work, and automatically code those sifted ones and make statistics after choosing the statistical mode. Table 6-1 is the statistical result:

Table 6-1   Statistics of Transitivity Concordance of *The Little Lame Prince*

Feature	Percentage/%	N
CLAUSES-TYPE	Sentence number=2021	
material	14.69	297
mental	11.87	240
verbal	19.94	403
relational	44.48	899
existential	4.70	95
behavioral	4.30	87

The research into the features of the interpersonal and textual metafunctions is expected to follow the methods brought up above though there are some variations in specific modeling and operation. Meanwhile, this method, of course, can be applied to crossing-texts study in the way to annotate and retrieve linguistic data collectively and simultaneously. Table 6-2 is the statistical result of annotating another three narrative texts and crossing-texts retrieval.

Table 6-2   Crossing-texts Statistics of Syntactical Annotation and Concordance

System	Feature	Count	Mean/%
Process	material	48, 28, 54	77.4, 71.8, 57.4
	behavioural	5, 3, 6	8.1, 7.7, 6.4
	verbal	3, 1, 13	4.8, 2.6, 13.8
	mental	3, 4, 5	4.8, 10.3, 5.3
	relational	3, 3, 15	4.8, 7.7, 16.0
	existential	0, 0, 1	0, 0, 1.1
Subject	boy,decker,decker	14, 13, 53	22.6, 33.3, 56.4
	dog,budd,budd	3, 11, 17	4.8, 28.2, 18.1
	boy+dog, other-subject, other-subject	22, 15, 24	35.5, 38.5, 25.5
	Frog	21	33.9
	other agents	2	3.2
Voice	active	62, 33, 90	100.0, 84.6, 95.7
	passive	0, 6, 4	0, 15.4, 4.3

The elaboration and illustration of the annotation and concordance above suggest that the annotation, the concordance and the following analysis in the corpus-supported approach to SFG are set under the framework of SFG, namely, SFG is the guideline, without which, there is no corpus-supported approach to SFG. Whether a single-text corpus research or a crossing-texts corpus research is presented, saving time and labor is the key to all the other aspects of research. Meanwhile, clauses are not fully annotated, that is, not the whole picture of the theoretical framework in SFG is marked in corpus data because more space is expected to leave for the observation beyond SFG. Only through this way, can the semi-automatic/automatic annotation be realized. The corpus-supported approach is progressed, instead of being confined, by SFG. The present manual annotation has come to a stop because it is too costly to continue, and the ensuing small-scale corpus or *archives* shows less value in linguistic research. The highly automatic annotation in CL suggests that there is a way to annotate grammar from the lexical pole. Though representing grammar in the form of a lexical regex is indirect and needs a long way to go, this approach is worth penetrating into because linguistic data in the corpus are comparatively more easily annotated and retrieved than that done from the grammatical pole.

The corpus-supported approach to SFG is the study based on the real linguistic proof, and it describes and explains linguistic forms, meaning and functions through the attested data and the statistical method. It is an incorporation of the ideas of CL into SFG research and belongs to the extended complementary branch of the grand system of SFG. And not all SFG studies are too grammar-heavy to recognize the lexical preference in CL. The lexico-grammatical construction of meaning originates from the lexical potential choices, and construing modes in lexico-grammar are essentially the probabilistic patterns formed in the choice. In addition, being too SFG-heavy will disobey the natural qualities of the corpus and CL in the attestation with a large amount of the natural linguistic data and bias the objectivity, because the SFG-heavy annotation affects research result previously with the small-scaled corpus and the researchers' prejudiced ideas. The conventionality of the real usage of lexical-grammar can be established into the probabilistic profile attained by observing the vertical linear co-occurring functions of the systemic potential lexical choice, which is the basis of setting up the syntactical probabilistic profile in both the single-text and crossing-texts approaches. Meanwhile, the corpus-supported approach to SFG will refine and advance the development of SFG. "In the longer term, the accumulation of evidence from corpus studies will yield a more coherent account of the nature of language, revealing each language as a metastable system which is variable in time, in space and in its context of use (diachronic, dialectal, and register, or diatypic, variation)" (Halliday 2008: 75). The approach is worth exploring into because it promotes the theoretical research in CL, "Designing, building, managing and interrogating a corpus are all highly theoretical activities. And, for that very reason, the corpus also provides the foundation for some highly practical outcomes, like the COBUILD series of reference works edited by John Sinclair " (Halliday 2008: 76).

6.3 Summary

What is most concerned about the realization of the corpus-supported approach to SFG is to annotate the grammatical information in SFG in the corpus for concordance. The marking of the ideational metafunction is featured with its unique theoretical modeling and application. Generally, the primary task of the annotation in the corpus-supported approach to SFG is to put the question to be researched into under the framework of SFG. The modeling of the theories in SFG into retrievable patterns or strings contains the specific steps as follows:

1) Set the concrete content at certain level of research, such as one of the three metafunctions.

2) Specify the research question and formalize it into certain structure, a logical form or a structural pattern, which is tried to be edited into a regex, and the key to the transformation is that the necessary linguistic features must be fully represented in the patterned strings and the ultimate transformed regex. The full representation is the assurance of objectivity and comprehensiveness of the

final research results.

3) Concordance according to the regex edited from formalization of the linguistic features characteristic of the research question, and the key to retrieval is to find the proper concordance tool that supports the edited regex.

4) Sift the concordance lines manually, checking whether all the retrieved lines are the required ones, and ticking off those that are not fully agree with what the regex requires. There is the need for a manual sifting because the regex is a formalized retrieval, while what we try to analyze is from the perspective of meaning.

5) Collectively annotate those that represent certain linguistic feature(s) with the marking names from the framework of SFG.

6) Set or design statistical items according to the research purpose after attaining retrieval and annotation.

In addition, the modeling guidelines must be put in practice of annotating linguistic data in the corpus. With the combination of the software of *Wordsmith* and *UAM CorpusTool*, the annotation operation is realized by the following measures:

1) tag all texts or the corpus with CLAWS;

2) retrieve the predicate verbs with Concordance Tool;

3) make a list of words of the retrieved predicate verbs with Wordlist Tool of *Wordsmith*;

4) establish the thesaurus of the researched aspect of SFG from the word list of a text or the corpus;

5) set and design the retrieving program and the set thesaurus into the retrieving wild card(s) or more inclusive regex;

6) put the texts or the corpus into the *UAM CorpusTool*;

7) readjust or design an annotating scheme according to the research and the framework of SFG;

8) put in the scheme;

9) retrieve first by the regex edited for the required data in the research;

10) sift the concordance lines manually to tick off and delete all that does not agree with the regex at the meaning level, and if necessary, add some more

changes to the annotating scheme, the thesaurus, or the regex when considering some exceptions are valuable;

11) annotate all the checked concordance nodes automatically with the concepts in the annotating scheme.

Chapter Seven

A Corpus-Supported Approach to the Textual Metafunction

In the corpus-supported approach to SFG, the penetration into cohesion also abides by the principle of lexical preference in CL, because the automatic process of linguistic data begins more with the lexical pole than the grammatical one.

7.1 A Corpus Approach to the Cohesion System in SFG

Cohesion is more lexical because it is mainly represented in a single word like *and, but, or,* or a set combination of words like *in addition to, that is to say, to get back to the point.* Cohesion is described from a lexical point of view as part of the local textual functions of lexical items (Mahlberg 2006). A clear definition of cohesion is the precondition for moving further on this topic. In Halliday and Hasan's (1976: 299) words, "…cohesion expresses the continuity that exists between one part of the text and another". Here cohesion is described as the crossing-clauses and crossing-paragraphs gluing device to form a whole text. Halliday (1998) moves more deeply into the gluing device and discovers that elaboration, extension, and enhancement are also cohesive devices.

Later on, cohesion (Halliday & Matthiessen 2004: 532) is defined, in a broader and clearer sense, as a lexico-grammatical system above and below clauses in the textual metafunction of SFG and thus it plays the function of construing texts in its own dimension, "On the one hand, there is a set of lexico-grammatical systems that have evolved specifically as a resource for making it possible to transcend the boundaries of the clause, that is, the domain of the highest ranking grammatical unit. These lexico-grammatical systems originate in the textual metafunction and are collectively known as the system of COHESION". Here cohesion is a little different from the one proposed by Halliday and Hasan in 1976 in the elaboration on conjunction and its functions. Another point concerned in the ideas of Halliday in 2004 should be distinguished, in which the lexico-grammatical systems here exclude the thematic structure and informative structure that are considered to be logical in structuring texts. The cohesion in the broader definition regards cohesion more important as a way of the lexico-grammatical pattern in construing texts in a more comprehensive sense besides combining clauses logically and semantically.

Concluded from above, cohesion is a system of construing texts above clauses in a lexico-grammatical pattern. The cohesion is multidimensional and is represented by multiple patterns of different cohesive devices of distinctive meanings and functions. Cohesion is realized in two poles of the continuity of lexico-grammar and instantiated in both the grammatical and lexical forms. In the grammatical zone, cohesion is instantiated in the four forms of conjunction, reference, ellipsis and substitution; in the lexical zone, synonymy, hyponymy, repetition and collocation. Among all instantiating forms above, only conjunction runs across messages and it is more grammatical in form than meaning is. All the others are more lexical in form because they show less grammatical information, but more functions a lexical unit can play. Though conjunction is more grammatical, its instantiating forms or markers are more lexical like the clarification in the elaboration in conjunction. So generally speaking, cohesive devices defined in SFG are more lexical-preferring. Being more lexical-preferring suggests that this kind of linguistic data be processed more automatically. The modes and technology of CL may be a good reference.

In CL, a cohesive lexico-grammatical pattern is understood as a kind of co-selections of a lexical item, which is realized or created by a model which embraces the paradigmatic and syntagmatic dimensions of choice at each choice point. Sinclair (2004: 141-142) deals with the co-selection model from the five categories serving as components of a lexical item. Among the five, two are obligatory; three, optional. The first obligatory one is the core that is invariable and constitutes the evidence of the occurrence of the item as a whole; the other, semantic prosody, which is the determiner of the meaning of the whole. "The optional categories realize coordinated secondary choices within the item, fine-tuning the meaning and giving semantic cohesion to the text as a whole. The optional categories serve also as a means of classifying the members of a paradigm, and thus the two axes of patterning, the paradigmatic and the syntagmatic, are related; the relationship is in principle capable of automation, and is quantifiable" (Sinclair 2004: 141-142). The three optional categories that relate words together on dimensions are collocation, colligation and semantic preference. Collocation is syntagmatic in nature and it is the co-occurrence of words with no more than four intervening words in general understanding. Colligation is paradigmatic, and it is the co-occurrence of grammatical phenomena. On the syntagmatic axis our descriptive techniques at present confine us to the co-occurrence of a member of a grammatical class. Semantic preference is both syntagmatic and paradigmatic, and it is the restriction of regular co-occurrence to items which share a semantic feature. The three optional categories are related to each other in the increasing abstraction; collocation is concrete in the physical text, and it is the combination of specific words. Colligation is the collocation of word classes in which each specific word is just potential probabilistic choice. Semantic preference deals with the similarity of meaning which involves both collocation and colligation in semantic explanation.

7.2 Cohesion Research by the Corpus-Supported Approach to SFG

As is stated above, the instantiation of cohesion systems in texts is a kind of textual pattern that is more lexical-preferring. A model to learn cohesion systems with the support of corpora has been tentatively targeted and explored ever since the appearance of large corpora. Sinclair (1991) proposes that the application of corpora could be employed to make language learners more aware of the textual patterns and discover linguistic facts for themselves. Later on, Partington (1998: 89) pioneers into the cohesion study based on corpora and makes the point that, compared with a relatively great amount of research into lexis and syntax, there has been relatively less textual study based on corpora. He (1998: 89-106) advocates and practices the approach to combining wordlists and concordance lines for observation in context to make researchers to come closer to the patterns of textual cohesion. Yallop (2004: 61) points out that the access to modern corpora has made it possible to study texts far more intensively, and corpus linguists are now able to show the semantic cohesion of textual segments. Nesi and Basturkmen (2009: 26-27) observe the lexical bundles with the theory proposed by Hyland (2004) and explain that two of the three functions of lexical bundles in a text are the discourse organization (reflecting relationships between prior and coming discourse) and reference (referring to physical or abstract entities, or to the textual context), and they divide the second function into two categories: Category IIA and Category IIB. Category IIA is the topic introduction or focus represented by lexical bundles as it appears, and Category IIB is the topic elaboration or clarification.

7.2.1 A Corpus-Supported Approach to the Lexical Cohesion System

Let us come to the lexical cohesion system for more revealing ideas. Halliday and Hasan (1976) define lexical cohesion as reiteration and collocation. Reiteration is "the repetition of a lexical item, or the occurrence of a synonym of some kind, in the context of reference; that is, where the two occurrences have the same referent". (Halliday & Hasan 1976: 318-319). Later on as cohesion was more deeply penetrated into, "a synonym of some kind" in lexical cohesion proposed in 1976 was developed into synonymy & antonymy, and hyponymy & meronymy by Halliday and Hasan (1985, 1994). The characteristics of the lexical cohesion system determine the model, because the lexical cohesion should be designed in both the paradigmatic and syntagmatic dimensions. The concepts like repetition, synonymy & antonymy, and hyponymy & meronymy are paradigmatic because each of them can be retrieved by listing its members in a thesaurus. The syntagmatic dimension of the model for the lexical cohesion system is collocation serving as a cohesive device. Collocation is understood in SFG as "a word that is in some way associated with another word in the preceding text, because it is a direct repetition of it, or is in some sense synonymous with it, or tends to occur in the same lexical environment" (Halliday & Hasan 1976: 319). And here collocation is vague and abstract because collocation covers more than that understood at present in SFG and CL, that is, collocation covers synonymy & antonymy, and hyponymy & meronymy. Collocation has then been modified and simplified as follows, "… association between the items in question—a tendency to co-occur. This 'co-occurrence tendency' is known as collocation…clearly there is a semantic basis to a collocation of this kind". (Halliday 2004a: 576-577). Collocation here is defined as the co-occurrence with meaning basis; furthermore, collocation is described from the perspective of register, "Notice finally that collocations are often fairly specifically associated with one or another particular register, or functional variety of the language. This is true, of course; of individual lexical items, many of which we regard as 'technical' because they appear exclusively, or almost exclusively, in one kind of text. But it is also noteworthy that perfectly ordinary lexical items often appear in different collocations according to the text variety". (Halliday 2004: 577-578).

Meanwhile, Halliday quantifies the concept of collocation like this: "The measure of collocation is the degree to which the probability of a word (lexical item) increases the given presence of certain other word (the node) within a specified range (the span)." Registers provide the contexts in which lexical items collocate differently according to different varieties of texts. Later on, Halliday (2008: 38) illustrates the concept of collocation from the perspectives of quantity and probability in certain context, and the definition is as follows: "Firth had defined collocation as the company words keep; Sinclair and I saw this as a formal relation among lexical items that was manifested in quantitative terms. It was the extent to which the probability of a word is perturbed by the environment in which it is occurring: specifically, by the other words occurring around it, at least within a certain distance. The nature and extent of this distance remained to be empirically determined; our best guess was a span of four or five lexical words on either side of the node." Quantity is represented in the horizontal dimension realized as an association of a node with its collocates; probability is vertical because the realization of collocation is a choice from the potential lexis set.

Concluded from above, collocation can mean more senses in its two dimensions and multiple semantic relationships, which is the common ground for other lexical cohesive features to be represented. The model for the cohesion system research in the corpus-supported approach to SFG is the one through which the cohesive features in SFG are expected to be transformed into a lexical string or regex that can be automatically retrieved with frequency information. Furthermore, from the retrieved cohesive features and frequency, a statistical pattern is planned to be concluded to indicate the regularity or discovery in the cohesive system of a text, texts or a corpus. The key to the model is to make the cohesion system retrievable, that is, to lexicalize the features of the cohesion system in both grammatical and lexical zones into a concordance list or regex pattern. The other three relations of repetition, synonymy & antonymy, and hyponymy & meronymy can also be studied under the general framework of collocation in the paradigmatic dimension. The thesaurus of nodes in synonymy & antonymy, or hyponymy & meronymy can be set up for different research purposes. Here the thesaurus is to be understood in a broader sense, and it contains the lexical set of antonyms, hyponyms, meronyms of searched super-ordinate words besides synonyms. Once the thesaurus of a researched lexical feature is set up, then the members in the thesaurus are to be made in a list retrievable in certain format like *xml* or *txt* in the set concordance software. There are two problems to be solved before we put the model into practice. The first is which words are selected to represent the whole pattern of the lexical cohesion if no specific lexical cohesive device(s) is set; the other, how are the words found in a large corpus. Here the concepts of keyword and key keyword are proposed. The keyword here is different from the keyword in context, and the keywords in this section are defined in the statistical perspectives of frequency and comparison and they are, in a text(s) or a corpus, statistically significant and more frequent than expected when compared with a corpus which is of larger or equal size.

Usually log-likelihood[①] or the chi-squared test[②] is used to compare two word lists in order to derive keywords. The common keywords include 1) proper nouns; 2) grammatical words suggesting a particular stylistic profile; 3) lexical words that give an indication of the 'aboutness' of a text (Baker, Hardie & McEnery 2006: 97-98). Key keywords are also distinguished from the ones in CL and they are evaluated from the relatedness of keywords with the research topic.

Several steps are taken to apply this model to lexical cohesion in the corpus-supported approach to SFG as follows:

1) set the research topic within lexical cohesion, such as any one of the four kinds, a feature of one kind, or four kinds as a whole;

2) lexicalize the cohesive features for research into a list form, like setting up the thesaurus of a cohesive feature of synonymy by listing all the synonyms of a super-ordinate of a thesaurus;

3) all the lexicalized features completed, each feature should be allotted a concordance list, and if necessary, some contextual word lists are expected to be given;

4) transform a text or a corpus into the format that can be recognized by concordance software, like *txt*;

5) select proper concordance software like *Wordsmith, Concordance, AntConc*, and put in the file as concordance source and the nodes for retrieval;

6) observe the retrieved results and the statistical format to draw a conclusion.

In the following, we cite three long texts as the research subject and all the other texts in the corpus as the reference or background information to see the cohesive pattern or regularity characteristic of a minute level of a register.

---

① Log-likelihood is a test for statistical significance, and it is sometimes called G-square or G score. It compares the observed and expected values for two datasets and uses a different formula to compute the statistic that is used to measure the difference. (Baker, Hardie & McEnery 2006: 109).

② The chi-squared test is a test for determining the significance of any numeric difference observed in data. The chi-squared test compares the difference between the observed values (e.g. the actual frequencies extracted from corpora) and the expected values (e.g. the frequencies that one would expect if no factor other than chance was affecting the frequencies). The greater the difference between the observed values and the expected values, the less likely it is that any difference is due to chance. Conversely, the closer the observed values are to the expected values, the more likely it is that the difference has arisen by chance (Baker, Hardie & McEnery 2006: 31).

The corpus here is *Children's Corpus* and it contains more than one million words. And the three texts selected from the corpus as the target of research are *Alice in Wonderland* (30,602 words), *Beauty and the Beast* (87,112 words), and *The Golden Road* (78,810 words), and the total number of words of the texts reaches nearly 200,000 (196,524) words with a reference corpus with nearly one million words. The lexical cohesive pattern of key words is expected to be found and set up from the corpus. Let us make the reference wordlist, which is the background to foreground the key words that distinguish a specified text from others. According to the processing principle in the corpus, a reference corpus is no less than the target text investigated. Here we get a reference corpus of nearly 200,000 words cited from the same corpus. The software used here is *Wordsmith*. The first step is to make the reference wordlist from *Children's Corpus*, and it is made as follows (The reference is shown partially).

WordSmith Tools — 2011-5-29 10:01:17

N	Word	Freq.	%
1	THE	5,553	4.37
2	AND `	4,178	3.29
3	TO	3,245	2.56
4	A	2,947	2.32
5	OF	2,651	2.09
6	I	2,369	1.87
7	HE	2,026	1.60
8	IT	1,972	1.55
9	WAS	1,833	1.44
10	IN	1,673	1.32
11	THAT	1,569	1.24
12	YOU	1,431	1.13
13	SHE	1,328	1.05
14	HIS	1,304	1.03
15	HER	1,263	0.99
16	HAD	1,110	0.87

17	FOR	1,028	0.81
18	BUT	1,025	0.81
19	AS	941	0.74
20	WITH	937	0.74
...			

Next, make wordlists of the three texts, and we take the part of the wordlist of *Alice in the Wonderland* for a sample to demonstrate the process.

WordSmith Tools — 2011-5-29 10:45:25

N	Word	Freq.	%
1	THE	7,195	4.68
2	AND	5,050	3.29
3	TO	3,974	2.59
4	A	3,579	2.33
5	OF	3,165	2.06
6	I	2,779	1.81
7	IT	2,502	1.63
8	WAS	2,190	1.42
9	HE	2,146	1.40
10	IN	2,042	1.33
11	SHE	1,869	1.22
12	THAT	1,849	1.20
13	YOU	1,796	1.17
14	HER	1,511	0.98
15	HIS	1,400	0.91
16	HAD	1,288	0.84
17	AS	1,204	0.78
18	BUT	1,195	0.78
19	FOR	1,181	0.77
20	SAID	1,166	0.76
...			

And then the reference wordlist and wordlists of the texts for investigation are put in the *WordSmith* to produce the keyword lists. The keyword list below of the first text is taken to indicate the all.

WordSmith Tools — 2011-5-29 14:12:04

N	WORD	FREQ.	ALICEI~1.TXT%	FREQ.	REFER.	LST%	KEYNESS P
1	ALICE	386	1.45	390	0.36	346.1	0.000000
2	SAID	462	1.73	969	0.90	123.0	0.000000
3	THE	1,642	6.15	4,934	4.59	105.4	0.000000
4	SHE	541	2.03	1,436	1.34	64.7	0.000000
5	KING	61	0.23	63	0.06	53.1	0.000000
6	QUEEN	68	0.25	79	0.07	51.7	0.000000
7	TURTLE	57	0.21	57	0.05	51.3	0.000000
8	MOCK	6	0.21	56	0.05	50.4	0.000000
9	HATTER	55	0.21	55	0.05	49.5	0.000000
10	GRYPHON	55	0.21	55	0.05	49.5	0.000000
11	HERSELF	83	0.31	124	0.12	44.3	0.000000
12	RABBIT	47	0.18	47	0.04	42.3	0.000000
13	BEGAN	58	0.22	74	0.07	39.1	0.000000
14	MOUSE	43	0.16	44	0.04	37.8	0.000000
15	DORMOUSE	39	0.15	39	0.04	35.1	0.000000
16	DUCHESS	38	0.14	38	0.04	34.2	0.000000
17	VERY	144	0.54	315	0.29	33.8	0.000000
18	OFF	73	0.27	119	0.11	33.5	0.000000
19	MARCH	34	0.13	37	0.03	27.9	0.000000
20	HARE	31	0.12	31	0.03	27.9	0.000000
21	AGAIN	83	0.31	158	0.15	27.8	0.000000
22	TONE	40	0.15	51	0.05	27.0	0.000000
23	VOICE	48	0.18	73	0.07	24.9	0.000001
24	CATERPILLAR	27	0.10	27	0.03	24.3	0.000001
25	REPLIED	29	0.11	31	0.03	24.3	0.000001
26	HOUSE	18	0.07	210	0.20	25.4	0.000000

27	LIFE	12	0.04	177	0.16	28.0	0.000000
28	ME	68	0.25	523	0.49	29.9	0.000000
29	HOME	5	0.02	133	0.12	32.2	0.000000
30	I	410	1.54	2,231	2.08	34.4	0.000000
31	OLD	19	0.07	258	0.24	37.4	0.000000
32	MAN	5	0.02	148	0.14	37.8	0.000000
33	HAS	7	0.03	179	0.17	42.4	0.000000
34	HIM	43	0.16	442	0.41	44.7	0.000000
35	HE	120	0.45	1,013	0.94	72.0	0.000000
36	MISS	4	0.01	270	0.25	91.1	0.000000

Next, we analyze the keyword lists to decide on the key keywords for the research according to the evaluation of each word in its relatedness to the topic to be investigated. The keyword list above is observed to select the key keywords for the study on the lexical cohesive research (the words indicate grammatical research is to be coped with in the later section). That is, here we deal mainly with the repetition, synonymy & antonymy, or hyponymy & meronymy. Based on this principle, the pronouns and conjunctions (both kinds are grammatical cohesion) are excluded. Then we set up a thesaurus for each keyword from four kinds of lexical cohesion. The thesaurus is established with the help of the WordNet[1]. Here one point must be made clear that the inflected forms of a lemma are to be constructed as a thesaurus of repetition. The key keywords of *Alice in Wonderland* is taken for a demonstration. The key keywords are listed as follows: *said, king, queen, turtle, mock, hatter, gryphon, began, mouse, dormouse, duchess, very, off, march, hare, tone, voice, caterpillar, replied, house, life, me, home, old, man, has* and *miss*.

Parts of the thesauri of keywords are given as an illustration as follows:

---

[1] WordNet is a large lexical database of English. Nouns, verbs, adjectives and adverbs are grouped into sets of cognitive synonyms (synsets), each expressing a distinct concept.

Said: repetition thesaurus: say, says, saying

synonymy thesaurus: talk, utter, mouth, verbalize, sound;

......

Turtle: hyponymy thesaurus: (sea turtle and marine turtle (snapping turtle, mud turtle terrapin (red-bellied terrapin and yellow-bellied terrapin)...));

meronymy thesaurus: (carapace, shell, cuticle, shield)

......

Old: synonymy thesaurus: (aged, aging, senior, elderly, antique, antiquated, archaic, obsolete)

antonymy thesaurus: (young, immature, new, former)

......

After all the thesauri of the three texts have been set up, each key keyword with its thesaurus members is to be retrieved in the text in which it occurs for the first time. For the repetition thesaurus, a regex like lemma* is to be used for all the inflected forms of the original word. Some of the key keywords with their thesauri of *Alice in Wonderland* are retrieved as follows:

WordSmith Tools — 2011-5-31 9:08:51

N	Concordance	Set	Tag	Word No.	File	%
1	'But I'm NOT a serpent, I tell you!' said Alice. 'I'm a--I'm a--' 'Wel			10,443	h:\alicei~1.txt	38
2	hat sort of a dance is it?' 'Why,' said the Gryphon, 'you first form into a			20,855	h:\alicei~1.txt	77
3	empt proved a failure. Alice heard it say to itself 'Then I'll go round and ge			7,148	h:\alicei~1.txt	26
4	upted in a great hurry. 'You did!' said the Hatter. 'I deny it!' said			24,045	h:\alicei~1.txt	89
5	'It is a very good height indeed!' said the Caterpillar angrily, rearing i			9,649	h:\alicei~1.txt	35
6	ll you a couple?' 'You are old,' said the youth, 'and your jaws are too w			9,367	h:\alicei~1.txt	34
7	?' 'It matters a good deal to ME,' said Alice hastily; 'but I'm not lookin			10,650	h:\alicei~1.txt	39
8	a porpoise.' 'Wouldn't it really?' said Alice in a tone of great surprise.			21,787	h:\alicei~1.txt	81
9	e face. 'I'll put a stop to this,' she said to herself, and shouted out, 'You'			7,942	h:\alicei~1.txt	29

N	Concordance	Set	Tag	Word No.	File	%
10	me as if he had a bone in his throat,' said the Gryphon: and it set to work sh			20,752	h:\alicei~1.txt	77
11	make you a present of everything I've said as yet.' 'A cheap sort of pres			19,131	h:\alicei~1.txt	71
12	e must have a prize herself, you know,' said the Mouse. 'Of course,' the Do			5,247	h:\alicei~1.txt	19
13	you know about this business?' the King said to Alice. 'Nothing,' said Ali			25,021	h:\alicei~1.txt	93
14	entures--beginning from this morning,' said Alice a little timidly: 'but it's			21,863	h:\alicei~1.txt	81
15	y.' 'I'm afraid I don't know one,' said Alice, rather alarmed at the propo			14,904	h:\alicei~1.txt	55
16	to see you again, you dear old thing!' said the Duchess, as she tucked her arm			18,419	h:\alicei~1.txt	68
17	again. That's all.' 'Thank you,' said Alice, 'it's very interesting. In			21,574	h:\alicei~1.txt	80
18	eady to agree to everything that Alice said; 'there's a large mustard-mine near			18,941	h:\alicei~1.txt	70
19	usic.' 'Ah! that accounts for it,' said the Hatter. 'He won't stand beati			14,487	h:\alicei~1.txt	53
20	Alice remarked. 'Right, as usual,' said the Duchess: 'what a CLear way you			18,906	h:\alicei~1.txt	70
21	name is Alice, so please your Majesty,' said Alice very politely; but she added			16,501	h:\alicei~1.txt	61
22	K,' said Alice. 'Of course it is,' said the Duchess, who seemed ready to ag			18,929	h:\alicei~1.txt	70
23	pose"?' said Alice. 'I mean what I say,' the Mock Turtle replied in an offe			21,833	h:\alicei~1.txt	81
24	half to Alice. 'What IS the fun?' said Alice. 'Why, SHE,' said the Gr			19,726	h:\alicei~1.txt	73
25	aid Alice. 'Why, there they are!' said the King triumphantly, pointing to			25,994	h:\alicei~1.txt	97
26	d of being all alone here!' As she said this she looked down at her hands,			3,205	h:\alicei~1.txt	12
27	'What CAN all that green stuff be?' said Alice. 'And where HAVE my shoulde			10,081	h:\alicei~1.txt	37
28	nd fidgeted. 'Give your evidence,' said the King; 'and don't be nervous, or			23,659	h:\alicei~1.txt	88
29	about again, and Alice heard the Rabbit say, 'A barrowful will do, to begin wit			7,890	h:\alicei~1.txt	29
30	owed and smiled in reply. 'Idiot!' said the Queen, tossing her head impatie			16,475	h:\alicei~1.txt	61

Then we retrieve the collocations of each thesaurus to see the keywords' repetition frequency and collocates (only keywords with the total frequency higher than 44 are listed.):

WordSmith Tools — 2011-5-31 10:18:58

N	WORD	TOTAL	LEFT	RIGHT	L10	L9	L8	L7	L6	L5	L4	L3	L2	L1	R1	R2	R3	R4	R5	R6	R7	R8	R9	R10
1	SAID	632	84	86	14	8	11	16	12	7	11	1	3	1	11	1	2	10	5	11	15	11	6	14
2	THE	528	224	304	21	18	21	25	25	20	14	35	45	0	35	22	17	28	32	31	40	39	34	26
3	I	282	145	137	17	16	13	15	17	15	16	12	17	7	16	11	19	16	11	12	12	8	16	16
4	TO	281	150	131	18	16	15	14	16	11	11	15	12	22	13	11	6	11	16	18	15	16	19	6
5	A	258	121	137	20	7	11	14	12	12	23	13	9	0	7	20	14	19	19	9	11	11	12	15
6	YOU	234	142	92	10	15	12	13	14	12	20	17	15	14	6	7	9	13	9	9	11	11	9	8
7	AND	225	89	136	15	9	11	6	4	8	4	5	9	18	12	12	28	12	5	12	12	17	15	11
8	IT	225	132	93	16	8	10	14	10	10	10	15	18	21	9	3	13	14	7	12	7	13	3	12
9	ALICE	167	82	85	9	9	5	10	11	6	9	9	3	11	12	11	10	6	8	3	9	8	11	7
10	OF	157	89	68	5	9	14	8	4	10	9	15	8	0	8	4	3	4	9	11	7	3	7	12
11	SHE	133	69	64	4	2	3	8	6	4	4	4	1	35	9	8	10	8	7	5	8	0	3	6
12	IN	111	46	65	5	4	7	3	2	2	6	8	4	1	5	9	11	10	4	3	6	6	7	4
13	THAT	105	59	46	5	5	5	2	5	8	11	5	7	6	4	0	6	5	4	5	8	2	6	6
14	AS	90	39	51	4	6	2	3	2	2	5	2	13	0	6	4	9	3	2	4	7	4	5	7
15	WAS	87	42	45	2	7	5	1	2	4	9	5	3	4	7	3	4	3	6	4	4	7	5	2
16	SAY	78	13	14	3	0	3	4	0	0	1	1	0	1	2	0	0	1	1	2	2	3	1	2
17	WHAT	78	50	28	3	5	6	4	5	5	8	5	7	2	4	3	1	4	4	3	2	2	2	4
18	AT	74	36	38	2	4	4	3	2	8	5	3	5	0	5	1	2	6	2	5	5	3	4	5
19	NOT	73	39	34	4	1	3	2	5	3	5	6	4	6	2	7	7	4	5	3	3	4	3	2

N	WORD	TOTAL	LEFT	RIGHT	L10	L9	L8	L7	L6	L5	L4	L3	L2	L1	R1	R2	R3	R4	R5	R6	R7	R8	R9	R10
20	SO	72	27	45	3	4	3	1	2	3	1	2	3	5	6	2	6	2	6	5	3	6	5	4
21	WELL	69	36	33	2	1	4	6	4	3	6	2	3	5	2	2	6	2	2	2	6	4	4	3
22	HER	68	27	41	2	4	5	3	3	2	3	2	2	1	3	3	1	8	8	5	1	4	4	4
23	VERY	64	30	34	3	4	2	4	0	4	4	6	2	1	2	6	8	5	5	2	3	2	1	0
24	ALL	63	34	29	4	3	4	1	3	2	5	3	4	5	4	1	2	3	5	3	2	2	5	2
25	HE	63	37	26	2	2	4	6	2	2	0	3	3	13	2	29	4	7	4	2	1	0	3	3
26	KING	63	23	40	2	2	3	0	1	1	0	1	3	10	0	0	1	1	1	3	0	2	2	1
27	IS	62	35	27	1	2	3	2	6	3	3	12	1	2	4	0	4	3	3	3	2	3	3	2
28	BE	60	30	30	3	2	2	1	2	2	3	5	4	5	1	0	1	5	1	3	4	5	5	5
29	BUT	60	24	36	2	2	6	5	2	3	0	1	1	2	2	3	7	5	2	2	2	5	4	4
30	ON	55	23	32	1	0	3	5	5	2	0	0	4	3	3	1	3	5	2	3	4	3	6	3
31	KNOW	54	37	17	2	2	6	3	4	5	3	4	3	5	2	0	0	1	5	3	1	3	0	2
32	DON'T	53	30	23	4	2	5	1	2	2	3	8	3	0	0	0	5	5	4	2	0	2	4	1
33	WITH	52	23	29	1	2	2	4	2	2	2	3	3	2	3	1	6	3	1	4	5	0	4	2
34	FOR	49	24	25	4	3	5	1	3	3	1	1	2	2	1	1	2	3	4	2	2	3	6	1
35	I'M	49	26	23	2	2	5	3	4	3	4	2	2	0	2	2	3	3	1	2	2	4	1	4
36	YOUR	49	32	17	2	3	2	0	3	1	6	3	12	0	1	0	2	2	4	0	0	3	1	3
37	MOCK	47	15	32	0	1	1	2	3	1	2	0	3	0	2	20	1	0	0	0	2	3	1	2
38	DO	46	26	20	2	2	3	3	2	6	0	0	4	4	3	0	2	2	0	4	2	1	3	3
39	HATTER	44	11	33	2	2	1	0	1	0	2	1	0	2	0	21	1	0	1	1	1	5	3	0

......

Observed from the list above, we get the repetition frequency of the key keyword *say*, and the major patterns can thus be obtained. The repetition thesaurus of *say* occurs 532 times, and the frequency profile and the major repetition patterns are illustrated as follows according to the collocation list above.

1) Thesaurus frequency and percentage of *say*:

Total frequency:	532	Percentage
said	462	86.8
say	51	9.5
saying	15	2.8
says	4	0.75

2) According to L1 positions in the list, the repetition frequency and major foregrounding patterns are:

Repetition pattern	Frequency
to say	22
it said/says	21
and say	18
you said/say	14
she said/says	13
king says/said	10
I say	7

3) According to R1 positions in the list, the repetition frequency and major foregrounding patterns are:

Repetition pattern	Frequency
said/says/saying King	29
said/says Herself	24
said/say/saying the	22
said/says Hatter	21
said/ say/saying a	20
said/says Mock	20
said/ say you	20
said/says/saying caterpillar	18

said/says Gryphon	16
said/says Queen	12
said/ say/saying and	12
said/say I	11
said/say/saying to	11
said/says/saying Alice	11
said/says she	8
said/says/saying Dormouse	8

4) According to the positions from L10 to L2, the repetition and the major priming patterns are: (The order is from high to low and, for the omitted section, please refer to the above collocation list.)

Words	Left total frequence	Distribution from L10 to L2								
I	145	17	16	13	15	17	15	16	12	17
You	142	10	15	12	13	14	12	20	17	15
it 132		16	8	10	14	10	10	10	15	18
Alice	……									
She	……									
Her	……									
He	……									
King	……									
……										

5) According to the positions from R2 to R10, the repetition and the major priming patterns are (The order is from high to low and, for the omitted section, please refer to the above collocation list.):

Words		Right total frequency	Distribution from R2 to R10								
3	I	137	11	19	16	11	12	12	8	16	16
5	A	131	20	14	19	19	9	11	11	12	15
4	TO	137	11	6	11	16	18	15	16	19	6
6	YOU	92	7	9	13	9	9	11	11	9	8
7	AND	……									
8	IT	……									
9	ALICE	……									

10 OF ......

11 SHE ......

15 WAS ......

17 WHAT ......

20 SO ......

22 HER ......

......

Concluded from the four observations above, the thesaurus frequency profile and repetition pattern of *say* are described and explained as follows:

1) the past time inflection is the major form, taking up 86.8%, which indicates the process happens in the past;

2) the participants of the process *say* are *you, it, Alice, she, her, he, king* (for specific proportions, please refer to the above analysis), which suggests that, according to the frequency profile, *I* is the story-teller;

3) the contextual words indicating the process-occurring environments are the three main participants with their actions.

Next, we retrieve the synonymy thesaurus of *old*. We put in the concordance items like *aged/aging/senior, elderly/antique/antiquated/archaic/obsolete*, but we get no concordance entries found for the concordance items. That is to say, *old* is repeated for 19 times without any synonym. Then synonymy thesaurus of *say* is introduced in the form of *talk/utter/mouth/verbalize/sound* as in the following list.

WordSmith Tools — 2011-6-2 8:12:56

N	Concordance	Word No.	File	%
1	d be beheaded, and that you weren't to talk nonsense. The Queen's argument	18,268	h:\alicei~1.txt	67
2	vercome to do anything but sit with its **mouth** open, gazing up into the roof of	25,003	h:\alicei~1.txt	93
3	n?' said the Cat, as soon as there was **mouth** enough for it to speak with.	17,494	h:\alicei~1.txt	65
4	dry, he is gay as a lark, And will talk in contemptuous tones of the Shark,	22,191	h:\alicei~1.txt	82
5	ear! Do come back again, and we won't talk about cats or dogs either, if you d	4,232	h:\alicei~1.txt	15

N	Concordance	Word No.	File	%
6	it must be really offended. `We won't talk about her any more if you'd rather	4,011	h:\alicei~1.txt	14
7	that there was hardly room to open her **mouth**; but she did it at last, and mana	9,973	h:\alicei~1.txt	37
8	His voice has a timid and tremulous **sound**.] 'That's different from what	22,214	h:\alicei~1.txt	82
9	w here,' said the Dormouse. 'Don't talk nonsense,' said Alice more boldly:	23,819	h:\alicei~1.txt	89
10	en raised himself upon tiptoe, put his **mouth** close to her ear, and whispered '	16,969	h:\alicei~1.txt	63
11	ire Cat: now I shall have somebody to talk to.' 'How are you getting on?'	17,479	h:\alicei~1.txt	65
12	rumbling of little cartwheels, and the **sound** of a good many voices all talking	7,473	h:\alicei~1.txt	27
13	lame on others!' 'YOU'D better not talk!' said Five. 'I heard the Queen sa	15,996	h:\alicei~1.txt	59
14	pillar; and it put the hookah into its **mouth** and began smoking again. This	9,709	h:\alicei~1.txt	36
15	I do,' said the Hatter, 'you wouldn't talk about wasting IT. It's HIM.'	14,431	h:\alicei~1.txt	53
16	ed eagerly, for she was always ready to talk about her pet: 'Dinah's our cat.	5,852	h:\alicei~1.txt	22
17	o the end of his tail. 'As if I would talk on such a subject! Our family alw	4,039	h:\alicei~1.txt	14
18	my dear, and that makes you forget to talk. I can't tell you just now what th	18,601	h:\alicei~1.txt	69
19	han that,' said Alice. 'Oh, don't talk about trouble!' said the Duchess.	19,118	h:\alicei~1.txt	71
20	ed its arms, took the hookah out of its mouth again, and said, 'So you think yo	9,149	h:\alicei~1.txt	33
21	Caterpillar took the hookah out of its **mouth**, and addressed her in a languid, s	8,768	h:\alicei~1.txt	32
22	Caterpillar took the hookah out of its **mouth** and yawned once or twice, and shoo	9,738	h:\alicei~1.txt	36
23	es flat upon their faces. There was a **sound** of many footsteps, and Alice look	16,215	h:\alicei~1.txt	60
24	that I should think very likely it can talk: at any rate, there's no harm in	3,672	h:\alicei~1.txt	13
25	don't think--' 'Then you shouldn't talk,' said the Hatter. This piece	15,648	h:\alicei~1.txt	58
26	one listening, this time, as it didn't sound at all the right word) '--but I sh	709	h:\alicei~1.txt	3
27	ng, with its tongue hanging out of its **mouth**, and its great eyes half shut.	8,469	h:\alicei~1.txt	31
28	large canvas bag, which tied up at the **mouth** with strings: into this they slip	24,216	h:\alicei~1.txt	90

As is shown above, the total concordance lines reach 28, among which, 12 lines with bold nodes are sifted out manually because those marked ones do not abide by the entry conditions of the synonymy thesaurus of *say*. The lexical synonymy cohesion pattern of *say* is as follows:

1) the total occurence of synonyms of *say* is 15;

2) frequency distribution & percentage:

Keyword	Frequency	Percentage
talk	14	93
sound	1	7
mouth	0	0
speak	0	0
verbalize	0	0
utter	0	0

The other kinds of lexical relationship cohesion systems can be studied by following the three demonstrations above.

7.2.2 A Corpus-Supported Approach to the Grammatical Cohesion System

The model for the grammatical cohesion system in the corpus-supported approach to SFG is to transform the grammatical cohesion system into the lexical or phrasal patterns retrievable by concordance software. This transformation is made available by setting up the thesaurus of the specific grammatical cohesion.

7.2.2.1 Modeling Reference in the Corpus-Supported Approach to SFG

Grammatical cohesion includes reference, ellipsis, substitution and conjunction. Among them, detailed classifications exist. First, reference is the relationship in which one word is understood in reference to another. According to the different referring directions and positions where the referred words are, reference is divided into exophoric reference and endophoric reference. Exophoric reference means "that the identity presumed by the reference item is recoverable from the environment of the text…the reference links the text to its environment; but it does not contribute to the cohesion of the text, except indirectly when references to one and the same referent are repeated, forming a chain" (Halliday 2004a: 552). As the definition explains, exophoric reference points to something outside the text itself for reference, that is, to the environment, the situational context or social-cultural one for reference, so looking for the referring relationship through the corpus is impossible because concordance in the corpus is a way that is limited in the text for reference. Endophoric reference is defined (Halliday 2004a: 552) as follows:

> It means that the identity presumed by the reference item recoverable from within the text itself—or to be more precise, from the instantial system of meanings created as the text unfolds. As the text unfolds, speakers and listeners build up a system of meanings... Once a new meaning has been introduced, it becomes part of that system and is the right category of thing, it can be presumed by endophoric reference. There are actually two possibilities here. Endophoric reference may point 'backwards' to the history of the unfolding text, that is, to a referent that has already been introduced and is part of the 'text's system of meanings...This type of endophoric reference is called anaphora, or anaphoric reference, and the element that is pointed to anaphorically is called the antecedent. Anaphora is very common; it makes a significant contribution to many kinds of text... Alternatively, endophoric reference may point 'forwards' to the future of the unfolding text, that is, to a referent that is yet to be introduced... This type of endophoric reference is called cataphora, or cataphoric reference.

Both the cataphoric and anaphoric ones can find their referring objects respectively within texts and thus can be detected by concordance in the corpus.

Reference cohesion with its two kinds can be modeled with lexical preference, that is, to lexicalize the grammatical reference in the thesaurus. As is generally known, whether anaphoric and cataphoric, reference consists of personal and demonstrative ones. Personal reference can further be divided into personal pronouns and personal possessive pronouns. Similarly, demonstrative pronouns and determiners constitute demonstrative reference. All the four referring relationships in SFG are expected to be modeled into the lexicalized form that can be processed through the means in CL. The key to the applicability of this method is presupposed by two requirements: one is to be sure that the model must fully reflect the reference concept and meaning in SFG, which is the basis; the other is that the model is retrievable, otherwise, there is no corpus-supported approach. Therefore, modeling suggests lexicalizing the references in SFG into the retrieval thesaurus that the corpus-processing means support. According to SFG, personal pronoun is to be modeled as the thing/head reference thesaurus in which *he/him/his, she/her/hers, they/them/theirs* and *it* are members that are collectively representative of the personal determinative reference; the lexical model of a personal determiner is to set up the pre-determiner thesaurus which includes members like *his, her, its* and *their*. Demonstrative reference is the same, and two thesauri are to be established to lexicalize this reference: the head/thing demonstrative thesaurus includes members of *this/these, that/those*, and *it* representative of pronoun reference in this sense; pre-modifier demonstrative constitutes of another thesaurus are *this/these, that/those*, and *the* (determiner); head demonstrative thesaurus, *here* and *there*. All the thesauri of personal reference can be listed as follows:

1) thing/head determinative personal reference thesaurus: *I/me/mine, we/us/ours, you/yours, he/him/his, she/her/hers, they/them/theirs, it;*

2) pre-determiner possessive personal reference thesaurus: *my, our, your, his, her, its, their;*

3) head/thing demonstrative pronoun personal reference thesaurus: *this/these, that/those, it;*

4) pre-modifier demonstrative determiner thesaurus: *this/these, that/those, the;*

5) head demonstrative adverbial thesaurus: *here, there.*

There are two problems with this method. One is that members of each thesaurus intersect to some extent and thus the retrieved lines need a manual sifting to tick off those nodes that share the same form but do not conform to the entry conditions of the thesaurus investigated. The other is that the span in concordance cannot cover all referents even with the largest span set in retrieval because a few of referents can be found through a distance too long to be covered in texts by the concordance span. Manual sifting and setting proper span are the major prerequisites for this method. Word coverage in most sentences is from one to thirty, and here the proper span is set at fifteen for both right and left sides. There is another task required, that is, the possible referents should be certified through the wordlist, keyword list or key keyword list. These possible referents serve as the context words within the set span of nodes in concordance.

Let us give an operational illustration of this method, we still choose the text *Alice in Wonderland*. Thing/head determinative personal reference is the object to be investigated and the thesaurus is lexicalized in the retrieval items as: *I/me/mine/we/us/ours/you/yours/he/him/his/she/her/hers/they/them/theirs/it*. The possible referents gotten from the wordlist, collocation list, keyword list and key keyword list listed above are *Alice, king, queen, Gryphon, Hatter, Mock, mouse, Dormouse* and *turtle* that are rearranged as the context words. We load the text, put in the retrieval items and the context words, set the span (15R. 15L) and start the concordance.

WordSmith Tools — 2011-6-7 7:25:57

N	Concordance	Word No.	File	%
1	ourself!' 'I can't explain MYSELF, I'm afraid, sir' said Alice, 'because I	8,845	h:\alicei~1.txt	32
2	r to know your history, she do.' 'I'll tell it her,' said the Mock Turtle	19,886	h:\alicei~1.txt	73
3	t know it was YOUR table,' said Alice; 'it's laid for a great many more than th	13,766	h:\alicei~1.txt	51
4	or man, your Majesty,' he began. 'You're a very poor speaker,' said the Ki	24,163	h:\alicei~1.txt	90
5	f YOUR adventures.' 'I could tell you my adventures--beginning from this m	21,857	h:\alicei~1.txt	81

N	Concordance	Word No.	File	%
6	ake your choice!' The Duchess took her choice, and was gone in a moment.	19,309	h:\alicei~1.txt	71
7	finish your story!' Alice called after it; and the others all joined in chorus,	5,716	h:\alicei~1.txt	21
8	ell! WHAT are you?' said the Pigeon. 'I can see you're trying to invent somet	10,457	h:\alicei~1.txt	38
9	hat happened to you? Tell us all about it!' Last came a little feeble, squ	7,758	h:\alicei~1.txt	28
10	TO YOU,'" said Alice. 'Why, there they are!' said the King triumphantly, p	25,993	h:\alicei~1.txt	97
11	ou think you're changed, do you?' 'I'm afraid I am, sir,' said Alice; 'I ca	9,160	h:\alicei~1.txt	34
12	ow you're growing too.' 'Yes, but I grow at a reasonable pace,' said the D	23,832	h:\alicei~1.txt	89
13	, whether you're nervous or not.' 'I'm a poor man, your Majesty,' the Hatte	23,935	h:\alicei~1.txt	89
14	ter, 'or you'll be asleep again before it's done.' 'Once upon a time there	14,981	h:\alicei~1.txt	55
15	e Duchess: you'd better ask HER about it.' 'She's in prison,' the Queen s	18,327	h:\alicei~1.txt	68
16	ing to draw, you know—' 'What did they draw?' said Alice, quite forgetting	15,311	h:\alicei~1.txt	56
17	'Why did you call him Tortoise, if he wasn't one?' Alice asked. 'We ca	20,069	h:\alicei~1.txt	74
18	d you fellows were saying.' 'Tell us a story!' said the March Hare. '	14,955	h:\alicei~1.txt	55
19	ce, 'and why it is you hate--C and D,' she added in a whisper, half afraid tha	5,443	h:\alicei~1.txt	20
20	tter, 'you wouldn't talk about wasting IT. It's HIM.' 'I don't know what	14,434	h:\alicei~1.txt	53

......

And then the concordance lines can be fully observed by setting the full show of the context of nodes in the Concordance Tool of *WordSmith* Tools.

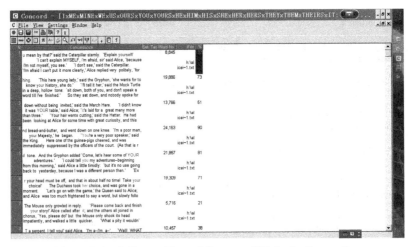

Figure 7-1　A Screen Shot of Context of Nodes in Concordance

Next, we can observe the plot of the retrieved items to get a general distribution and density of thing/head determinative personal reference pronouns.

Figure 7-2　A Screen Shot of Distribution and Density of Thing/Head Determinative Personal Reference Pronouns

Next, the collocation list is made to see the referents and the reference between the thing/head determinative personal reference pronouns and the referents.

WordSmith Tools — 2011-6-7 7:31:38

N	WORD	TOTAL	LEFT	RIGHT	L15	L14	L13	L12	L11	L10	L9	L8	L7	L6	L5	L4	L3	L2	L1	R1	R2	R3	R4	R5	R6	R7	R8	R9	R10	R11	R12	R13	R14	R15
1	THE	2979	1436	1543	99	105	120	106	115	112	122	81	97	111	91	102	144	31	0	1	73	162	108	108	112	115	103	113	114	109	104	102	112	107
2	SAID	1363	642	721	45	51	46	46	55	47	36	37	42	40	55	91	39	9	3	22	86	49	47	48	57	52	64	47	51	36	40	46	47	29
3	AND	1315	672	643	42	46	45	47	43	50	43	43	45	35	42	53	39	35	64	0	62	29	38	50	51	43	35	55	38	43	55	44	50	50
4	TO	1294	654	640	52	31	44	38	48	43	44	38	44	40	49	44	66	49	24	18	62	62	47	45	39	28	51	39	40	41	39	46	47	36
5	ALICE	1280	684	596	47	52	44	47	50	51	42	45	50	39	41	44	47	76	9	1	24	54	41	45	46	45	51	42	44	50	34	48	42	29
6	I	1251	543	455	33	33	37	28	25	39	26	25	31	29	27	24	45	38	103	8	30	25	32	38	41	34	33	33	26	28	34	36	35	27
7	IT	1206	472	437	29	35	30	36	23	29	33	35	43	34	34	22	28	26	35	5	24	47	28	26	33	27	25	29	31	26	42	22	32	40
8	A	1143	541	602	46	38	34	38	28	41	46	37	43	47	42	50	34	17	0	6	55	37	38	43	51	42	40	39	44	44	44	37	30	44
9	YOU	1085	452	394	29	33	34	28	26	28	23	34	34	38	23	22	28	30	42	2	24	26	26	32	28	30	27	26	36	36	29	30	30	21
10	SHE	871	274	374	22	14	19	20	25	16	17	21	14	22	26	18	20	16	4	6	13	17	27	28	21	27	30	28	32	25	26	34	35	25
11	OF	766	428	338	30	40	28	33	21	25	19	24	35	30	30	35	23	16	39	0	16	17	26	37	28	22	25	17	23	28	21	27	30	21
12	IN	656	318	338	25	14	20	23	26	28	21	21	26	23	23	27	16	5	20	9	16	20	20	31	29	25	15	33	27	19	19	21	25	25
13	WAS	581	258	323	16	20	20	16	23	18	15	19	26	23	25	18	15	5	4	62	7	13	16	14	16	18	20	18	25	20	19	25	22	28
14	AS	508	287	221	10	13	14	17	17	15	15	17	22	15	13	21	22	13	63	6	15	19	16	14	17	11	15	16	15	19	9	15	12	25
15	THAT	489	267	222	15	16	16	17	26	14	22	17	18	16	18	14	5	10	43	1	13	11	10	18	17	17	15	14	16	21	21	12	21	17
16	HER	451	150	175	6	12	10	7	10	16	6	7	14	12	11	13	13	11	2	2	8	13	11	14	13	8	12	13	15	16	13	13	13	17
17	AT	404	194	210	11	12	15	10	16	10	17	10	8	8	11	18	14	6	19	5	11	9	14	19	14	12	21	12	16	20	14	14	19	19
18	ON	369	198	171	9	15	17	14	14	17	11	11	17	8	14	17	10	15	16	1	25	8	5	12	10	13	10	12	13	11	16	16	11	9
19	SO	351	182	169	12	18	12	9	13	12	12	12	9	9	12	14	9	6	27	5	13	15	10	12	6	13	9	11	16	12	11	10	10	10
20	WITH	345	171	174	13	9	12	8	7	12	11	17	13	10	8	16	7	5	23	4	8	12	10	9	11	15	10	19	12	9	15	15	17	10

N	WORD	TOTAL	LEFT	RIGHT	L15	L14	L13	L12	L11	L10	L9	L8	L7	L6	L5	L4	L3	L2	L1	R1	R2	R3	R4	R5	R6	R7	R8	R9	R10	R11	R12	R13	R14	R15
21	BUT	336	204	132	9	13	19	11	11	6	11	9	15	16	11	11	8	9	47	0	11	7	6	11	6	10	11	16	10	9	8	8	11	9
22	HE	323	136	111	7	10	10	16	8	11	7	5	12	9	13	4	11	7	6	1	9	8	5	18	4	8	6	6	5	8	6	6	9	8
23	ALL	313	149	164	9	7	7	9	9	10	13	10	6	10	13	11	11	6	14	13	8	5	12	10	10	13	11	19	5	5	11	10	8	15
24	THEY	306	116	109	12	9	9	9	9	11	6	5	5	6	8	6	4	6	9	2	5	20	6	7	7	9	8	1	8	6	8	8	7	7
25	WHAT	304	169	135	6	13	10	8	8	9	8	10	15	13	10	12	9	15	21	2	16	14	7	7	15	8	10	11	8	8	10	7	7	5
26	HAD	302	135	167	9	8	11	6	11	15	10	12	12	12	5	5	7	8	2	42	16	8	4	8	8	9	12	9	8	9	10	7	6	7
27	VERY	293	133	160	10	10	7	10	16	6	13	8	9	7	13	9	20	6	6	4	6	12	14	8	8	12	6	12	15	15	9	5	14	10
28	NOT	284	125	159	8	7	7	7	8	9	11	9	9	8	13	5	5	6	3	0	25	9	12	6	11	10	10	21	6	7	11	5	7	11
29	KNOW	278	116	162	8	5	11	11	11	5	4	8	10	7	12	3	4	12	9	42	15	8	6	4	8	12	7	6	8	13	13	5	4	7
30	FOR	261	131	130	6	5	7	7	10	3	10	8	12	10	4	11	9	6	23	1	1	10	11	4	12	11	5	8	15	8	6	13	7	13
31	BE	245	119	126	8	10	9	9	8	6	8	9	10	7	11	12	10	5	1	2	25	8	12	10	14	7	6	6	8	7	8	9	7	12
32	HIS	244	98	84	6	3	8	8	8	6	10	7	7	6	7	7	6	5	1	1	2	4	7	4	5	10	6	3	2	7	7	7	9	8
33	IF	238	149	89	11	5	4	4	5	7	2	10	10	8	10	7	10	2	48	0	4	9	3	4	8	6	6	6	7	5	6	6	5	4
34	I'M	217	110	67	8	11	11	7	4	4	5	9	3	10	3	3	8	8	21	1	3	3	3	6	10	8	6	6	3	3	5	1	5	2
35	LIKE	217	104	113	11	7	7	3	4	9	6	7	6	6	10	5	10	4	6	10	14	6	7	9	6	9	10	5	8	8	10	7	3	8
36	THEM	214	78	87	6	6	7	1	11	5	6	6	9	9	5	4	5	5	3	0	5	6	6	6	5	8	7	6	2	11	6	5	6	6
37	THIS	213	113	100	10	10	11	7	5	5	9	9	6	10	5	5	8	16	6	1	0	6	5	7	14	4	13	9	6	10	10	7	7	6
38	THOUGHT	204	105	99	4	6	8	7	5	5	8	8	5	7	2	10	16	3	9	11	5	5	4	5	7	8	8	10	10	7	5	6	5	7
39	DON'T	200	86	114	2	9	5	5	2	6	8	8	7	7	8	5	4	8	1	29	2	7	5	8	6	6	4	9	5	7	8	7	9	5
40	WENT	200	90	110	9	9	8	8	9	6	5	7	5	4	6	3	12	1	0	2	1	2	3	6	6	10	8	9	6	8	6	6	11	8
41	IS	197	101	96	5	5	7	5	10	6	3	6	10	4	8	5	6	9	12	13	5	5	3	4	5	6	7	4	5	4	6	9	10	3
42	IT'S	191	89	64	7	9	3	7	4	4	4	3	4	3	9	3	6	4	23	0	5	1	2	4	5	6	5	8	4	4	7	7	2	6

...

The results of the lists and screen shots can be summarized in Tables 7-1, 7-2, 7-3, 7-4, which can suggest the overall patterns of thing/head determinative personal reference.

Table 7-1   Distribution and Proportion of Thing/Head Determinative Personal Pronouns

N	Word	Total	Proportion/%	Left	Right	Node
6	I (including 89 I'VE, 34 I'M, 172 I'LL &284 I'D)	1673	24.9	631	528	297
7	IT	1206	18.0	472	437	297
9	YOU	1085	16.2	452	394	239
10	SHE	871	13.0	274	374	223
16	HER	451	6.7	150	175	126
22	HE	323	4.8	136	111	76
24	THEY	306	4.6	116	109	81
32	HIS	244	3.6	98	84	62
36	THEM	214	3.2	78	87	49
51	ME	170	2.5	82	51	37
93	WE	105	1.6	52	30	23
258	US	31	0.5	10	12	9
287	MINE	27	0.4	9	10	8
771	YOURS	8	0.1	2	4	2
SUM		6714	100	2562	2406	1529

Table 7-2   Distribution and Proportion of the Referents Forming the Reference with Thing/Head Determinative Personal Pronouns

N	Word	Total	Proportion/%	Left	Right	Node
5	ALICE	1280	42.8	684	596	0
47	QUEEN	180	6.0	95	85	0
49	HATTER	175	5.9	93	82	0
52	GRYPHON	169	5.7	87	82	0
54	KING	164	5.5	77	87	0
57	MOCK	160	5.3	77	83	0
59	TURTLE	160	5.3	84	76	0
60	MOUSE	148	4.9	75	73	0

Continued

N	Word	Total	Proportion/%	Left	Right	Node
71	DORMOUSE	129	4.3	68	61	0
75	DUCHESS	120	4.0	60	60	0
91	CAT	105	3.5	56	49	0
128	RABBIT	72	2.4	34	38	0
130	HARE	71	2.4	41	30	0
147	CATERPILLAR	58	1.9	37	21	0
SUM		2991	100	1568	1423	0

Table 7-3   Distribution of Left Collocation

Left total	L15	L14	L13	L12	L11	L10	L9	L8	L7	L6	L5	L4	L3	L2	L1
684	47	52	44	47	50	51	42	45	50	39	41	44	47	76	9
95	8	7	8	6	3	2	11	3	2	12	4	10	7	12	0
93	6	6	2	3	7	7	10	6	8	6	5	1	5	18	3
87	7	4	8	10	5	8	3	7	2	4	6	2	7	14	0
77	8	7	5	4	4	8	3	5	5	5	5	4	5	9	0
77	4	4	2	8	9	8	5	4	6	3	11	8	5	0	0
84	8	3	3	3	7	10	8	5	3	6	4	10	8	6	0
75	7	5	6	5	7	7	8	4	6	6	4	0	5	3	2
68	9	3	5	3	2	7	4	11	7	3	2	5	4	3	0
60	4	1	3	6	3	8	5	7	4	2	5	2	3	5	2
56	8	3	2	5	6	3	6	2	5	1	4	3	0	7	1
34	1	3	2	5	2	4	0	1	6	1	2	1	2	2	2
41	5	5	1	3	1	4	1	2	3	2	2	5	3	4	0
37	2	3	5	2	1	0	3	3	2	2	2	4	5	3	0
Sum	124	106	96	110	107	127	109	105	109	92	97	99	106	162	19
Percentage	7.9	6.8	6.1	7.0	6.8	8.1	7.0	6.7	7.0	5.9	6.2	6.3	6.8	10.3	1.2

Table 7-4   Distribution of Right Collocation

Right total	R1	R2	R3	R4	R5	R6	R7	R8	R9	R10	R11	R12	R13	R14	R15
596	1	24	54	41	45	46	45	51	42	44	50	34	48	42	29
85	0	0	6	7	4	6	8	4	6	10	9	5	8	3	9
82	0	0	3	11	6	7	7	8	3	6	6	5	6	11	3
82	0	0	2	11	5	7	7	5	7	2	5	12	2	7	10
87	0	0	2	7	9	6	8	8	4	8	9	6	9	5	6
83	0	0	9	14	4	4	5	7	7	4	8	5	3	3	10
76	0	1	0	10	14	4	4	5	7	7	4	9	5	3	3
73	0	0	4	7	3	6	4	6	5	8	7	4	5	6	8
61	0	0	2	6	2	4	2	7	7	7	5	2	5	7	5
60	0	0	3	6	4	5	6	5	4	5	0	5	5	5	7
49	0	0	2	7	4	5	6	6	2	3	7	2	2	1	2
38	0	0	2	1	6	4	3	1	2	3	3	4	5	2	2
30	0	0	0	3	3	4	1	3	2	1	4	1	4	1	3
21	0	0	0	3	4	1	2	1	2	3	2	1	1	1	0
Sum	1	25	89	134	113	109	108	117	100	111	119	95	108	97	97
Percentage	0.1	1.8	6.3	9.4	7.9	7.7	7.6	8.2	7.0	7.8	8.4	6.7	7.6	6.8	6.8

The above tables can be decoded as follows:

1) The major thing/head determinative personal pronouns are: *I, it, you, she, her, he, they* (occurring frequency: above 300 or 4%). The less frequent pronouns are: *his, them, me, we* and *us* and the others are least frequent. This shows that the major reference pattern is the first personal pronominal active participants interwoven with the second personal pronominal active participants, and the third personal pronominal active participants are least frequent; active participants' personal pronouns account for the main proportion.

2) The proportion and distribution of context words suggest that *Alice* is the major referent, and *queen, Hatter, Gryphon, Mock* and *Turtle* occur almost with the same probabilities and distributions.

3) Concluded from the features of Tables 7-1 and 7-2, the major reference is the one between *Alice* and *I*. The less references are the ones between *Alice* and *she, queen* and *her, queen* and *she, duchess* and *she, duchess* and *her*, the references between *he* and *Hatter, he* and *king, he* and *Gryphon* and the ones between *it* and *rabbit*, and *it* and *hare*, *it* and *mouse*, *it* and *dormouse*, *it* and *Caterpillar, it* and infinitive and *it* and that-clause.

4) The distribution and proportion of referents (the context words) show that anaphoric references are a little more frequent than cataphoric ones. In anaphoric reference, L2 positions account for a large proportion, reaching the highest percentage of 10.3%; L10 and L15 (around 8%) are a little more frequent than L7, L9, L12 (around 7%); the other locations share almost the same proportion except the least frequent L1. In cataphoric reference, R4 position is the main position of referents (9.4%); R5–R8, R10–R11, and R13 positions vary little (around 8%); the other positions show the same tendency except R1–R2.

7.2.2.2 Modeling Conjunctions in the Corpus-Supported Approach to SFG

The cohesive system of conjunctions is logico-semantic and it contains two aspects, covering the cohesive devices between clauses and the ones between paragraphs. Halliday (2004a: 538) defines it like this: "The cohesive system of CONJUNCTION has evolved as a complementary resource for creating and interpreting text. It provides the resources for marking logico-semantic relationships that obtain between text spans of varying extent ranging from clauses within clause complexes to long spans of a paragraph or more" (Halliday 2004a: 542-544). The cohesive system of conjunctions is the system of the logico-semantic relationship of conjunction devices, and the classification of the conjunctions is dealt with. The cohesive system of conjunctions consists of elaboration, extension and enhancement with more detailed classification. Here elaboration is cited for an example:

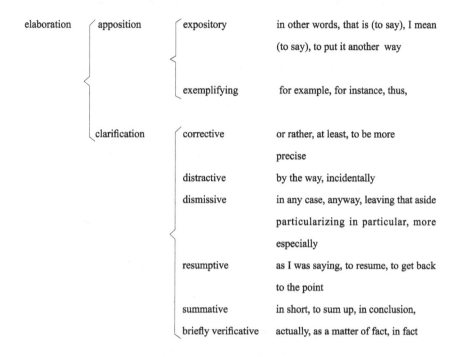

		expository	in other words, that is (to say), I mean (to say), to put it another way
elaboration	apposition		
		exemplifying	for example, for instance, thus,
	clarification	corrective	or rather, at least, to be more precise
		distractive	by the way, incidentally
		dismissive	in any case, anyway, leaving that aside
		particularizing	in particular, more especially
		resumptive	as I was saying, to resume, to get back to the point
		summative	in short, to sum up, in conclusion,
		briefly verificative	actually, as a matter of fact, in fact

The model for conjunctions in the corpus-supported approach to SFG is to rearrange these classifications into retrievable items for concordance. In this model, the first step is to determine which kind of conjunctions is to be researched into and then to find the words or phrases that can fulfill and represent the chosen kind. And then edit those chosen items into concordance forms acceptable by the set retrieving software. We still take the three texts, *Alice in Wonderland*, *Beauty and the Beast*, and *The Golden Road* for demonstration.

1) First, we choose all the three kinds of conjunctions for research, and divisions of enhancement conjunctions are partially chosen for demonstrative purpose. Next, we edit all the representative words or phrases into the retrievable forms.

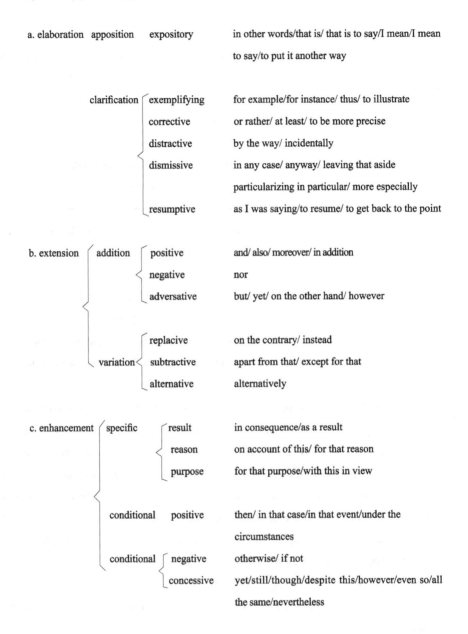

a. elaboration apposition expository — in other words/that is/ that is to say/I mean/I mean to say/to put it another way

clarification ⎰ exemplifying — for example/for instance/ thus/ to illustrate
corrective — or rather/ at least/ to be more precise
distractive — by the way/ incidentally
dismissive — in any case/ anyway/ leaving that aside
particularizing in particular/ more especially
resumptive — as I was saying/to resume/ to get back to the point

b. extension ⎰ addition ⎰ positive — and/ also/ moreover/ in addition
negative — nor
adversative — but/ yet/ on the other hand/ however

variation ⎰ replacive — on the contrary/ instead
subtractive — apart from that/ except for that
alternative — alternatively

c. enhancement ⎰ specific ⎰ result — in consequence/as a result
reason — on account of this/ for that reason
purpose — for that purpose/with this in view

conditional positive — then/ in that case/in that event/under the circumstances

conditional ⎰ negative — otherwise/ if not
concessive — yet/still/though/despite this/however/even so/all the same/nevertheless

2) Retrieve all those concordance strings of items in each of the three texts respectively and obtain the statistics of the results. To be specific, analyze the concordance lines, record the frequency of each feature in every one of the three texts respectively and make the frequency number of the same features

comparable by statistical means. An average per 1,0000 is taken in to make the concordance results comparable on the same par because the three texts are different in length.

Table 7-5   Distribution of Conjunctions

Type	Subtype	Sub-classification	Text 1	Average /10,000	Text 2	Average /10,000	Text 3	Average /10,000
elaboration	apposition	expository	10	3.3	10	1.1	29	3.7
		exemplifying	3	1.0	10	1.1	5	0.6
	clarification	corrective	1	0.3	14	1.6	3	0.4
		distractive	2	0.7	1	0.1	0	0.0
		dismissive	4	1.3	8	0.9	1	0.1
		particularizing	2	0.7	0	0.0	0	0.0
		resumptive	0	0.0	0	0.0	0	0.0
extension	addition	positive	874	285.6	3012	345.8	2,357	299.1
		adversative	215	70.3	743	85.3	708	89.8
	variation	replacive	3	1.0	23	2.6	9	1.1
		subtractive	0	0.0	0	0.0	0	0.0
		alternative	246	80.4	469	53.8	541	68.7
enhancement	specific	result	0	0.0	0	0.0	0	0.0
		reason	0	0.0	0	0.0	0	0.0
		purpose	0	0.0	0	0.0	0	0.0
		conditional:positive	3	1.0	2	0.2	1	0.1
		conditional:negative	5	1.6	7	0.8	4	0.5
		concessive	71	23.2	255	29.3	142	18.0

3) The concordance frequency pattern and comparable statistical pattern show that the three texts share similar configuration of the logico-semantic cohesive system of conjunction:

a. The three texts show similar proportions of elaboration apposition expository and exemplifying conjunction, and elaboration clarification particularizing and resumptive conjunction; the other subtypes of conjunction vary to some extent.

b. In extension conjunction, the frequencies of both the addition ones and variation subtractive and alternative ones are almost the same except that the replacive subtype is different across the three texts.

c. Enhancement conjunction illustrates that most subtypes are similar except that conditional negative and positive ones are different across texts.

d. Whether this configuration of similarity and difference is the conjunction pattern of the register of the texts still needs more data to attest.

7.3 Summary

The model for the cohesion system research in the corpus-supported approach to SFG is the one through which the cohesive features in SFG are to be transformed into the lexical strings and regexes that can be automatically retrieved with frequency information. The key to the model is to make the cohesion system retrievable, that is, to lexicalize the features of the cohesion system in both grammatical and lexical zones into a concordance list or regex pattern. In application, the core of formalizing cohesive system is to set up the thesaurus of nodes in synonymy & antonymy, or hyponymy & meronymy for different research purposes. Here the thesaurus is to be understood in a broader sense, and it contains the lexical set of antonyms, hyponyms, and meronyms of the searched super-ordinate words besides synonyms. Once the thesaurus of a researched lexical feature is set up, the members in the thesaurus are to be made in a list retrievable in certain format like *xml* or *txt* in the set concordance software. The condition for making the modeling effective is that the selected thesaurus members can be retrievable and fully represent the whole system of the lexical cohesion if there is no specific lexical cohesive device set. Several steps are taken to ensure the effect of applying this model to lexical cohesion in the corpus-supported approach to SFG as follows:

1) set the research topic within lexical cohesion, such as any one of the four kinds, a feature of one kind, or four kinds as a whole;

2) lexicalize the cohesive feature for research into a list form, like setting up the thesaurus of a cohesive feature of synonymy by listing all the synonyms

of a super-ordinate;

3) all lexicalized features completed, each feature should be allotted a concordance list, and if necessary, some contextual word lists are expected to be given;

4) transform a text or a corpus into the format that can be recognized by concordance software, like *txt*;

5) select a proper concordance software tool like *WordSmith*, *Concordance*, *AntConc* etc., and put in the file as concordance source and the nodes for retrieval;

6) observe the retrieved results and statistical format to make a conclusion.

In the corpus-supported approach to grammatical cohesion, it is essential that the collocation list and the thesaurus of cohesive features are to be made retrievable. As for both lexical and grammatical cohesion, the final research purpose is to be attained by observing the probability profile established from the statistic results of the comparative relative frequency of linguistic features within or across texts.

Chapter Eight

Conclusions

8.1 Summary of the Findings

The lexico-grammatical construction of meaning starts from the lexical potential choices, and the construing modes of lexico-grammar are essentially the probabilistic patterns formed in the choices of the lexical meaning from meaning potential. The regularity and conventionality of the real usage of lexical-grammar can be established into a probabilistic profile attained by observing the vertical linear co-occurring functions of the systemic potential lexical choices, which constitute the basis of setting up syntactical probabilistic profile both in the single-text research and crossing-texts research.

Based on the ideas above, a corpus-supported approach to SFG is proposed as a new way of incorporating corpora and CL into SFG research. SFG research based on corpora/corpus linguistics calls for a semi-automatic/automatic processing of a large amount of linguistic data in the corpus. It is neither the corpus-based approach nor the corpus-driven one. The corpus-supported approach makes the theories in SFG come closer to a large scale of linguistic data in the corpus. The corpus-supported approach makes the attestation to the linguistic theories and phenomena in SFG more objective and representative. In addition to the function of attestation, the approach is also applied to proposing a new linguistic supposition with the revealing concordance lines that are retrieved and shown in regularity. Theorizing on linguistic data is necessary and indispensable for both linguistic attestation and supposition, and theorization is the process to transform the theories in SFG into certain forms and patterns that can be retrieved and annotated in the corpus by some linguistic concordance and coding software. Furthermore, proper theorization is the key to the possible realization of the corpus-supported approach, in which large amounts of linguistic data are to be annotated in a semi-automatic/automatic way.

The mode for the semi-automatic/automatic annotation of the corpus is distinctive according to the different grammatical meaning that is to be marked in the corpus. The annotation of the grammatical information of the ideational metafunction in the corpus-supported approach is to mark the meaning at the clausal level with the marking realized in the lexical way, that is, to lexicalize the ideational meaning into some retrievable forms that can be concordanced automatically. The retrieved ideational meaning forms are to be sifted manually to exclude some exceptions, and then all the accepted meaning forms can be automatically marked at once. So the core of the process of marking the ideational meaning at the clausal level is to find and formalize the model lexicalizing the grammatical information of the ideational metafunction at the clausal level. Specifically speaking, retrieving and annotating the ideational metafunction take several steps in the realization: the first step is to set the concrete content of certain level of research, such as one of the three metafunctions; the second is to specify the research question and formalize the study question into the retrieval lexical and regex items, and raw data are to be retrieved with manual check; finally, the manually-sifted retrieved data are to be annotated collectively in an automatic way. The combination of the automatic annotation, concordance and manual sifting overcomes the disadvantages of being labor- and time-intensive. Several processes are to be followed to realize the automatic/semi-automatic process of linguistic data in the corpus in the corpus-supported approach to SFG: 1) tagging all texts or the corpus with certain software; 2) retrieving and making a list of the predicate verbs according to certain aspect of research with set software; 3) putting texts or the corpus into the software designed for SFG; 4) readjusting or designing the annotating scheme according to the research and framework of SFG; 5) loading in the scheme; 6) retrieving first by the regex edited for the required data in research and sifting the concordance lines manually to tick off and delete all the retrieved lines that do not agree to the regex at the meaning level, and if necessary, adding some more changes to the annotating scheme, the thesaurus, or regex when considering some exceptions are valuable; 7) annotating all the checked concordance nodes automatically with the concepts in the annotating scheme. In general, the theoretical modeling in the annotation of the ideational metafunction in the corpus-supported approach to SFG is essentially that the constituents in figures are lexicalized and patterned into the retrievable forms that can be annotated automatically/semi-automatically with the information of the ideational metafunction meaning. However, not all meanings of the ideational metafunction are modeled because the whole modeling biases the research result beforehand by confining the research completely under a pre-designed framework.

The model for the cohesion system research in the corpus-supported approach to SFG is somewhat distinctive from the research in the ideational metafunction, and it is more modeled than annotated, in which the cohesive system is made into the retrievable thesaurus and regex. To be specific, modeling the cohesion system of the textual metafunction is to transform the cohesion system into some lexical strings and regex that can be automatically retrieved. Specifically, formalizing the cohesive system is to set up the thesaurus of different cohesive meanings. The thesauri of synonymy, antonymy, hyponymy or meronymy for different research purposes are to be made in a list retrievable. Several steps are expected to be followed to ensure the realization of modeling cohesive system in SFG: 1) set the research topic within the cohesion system; 2) taking hyponymy as an example, set up the thesaurus of a cohesive feature of hyponymy by listing all the hyponyms of a super-ordinate or other relationships according to the set research; 3) allot each feature a concordance list, and if necessary, some contextual word lists are expected to be given; 4) observe the probability profile established from the statistic results of the comparative relative frequency of linguistic features within or across texts.

Though the corpus-supported approach to the ideational metafunction and the cohesive system is distinctive in modeling and formalizing theory, theorization on the observation of the retrieved linguistic data from the corpus holds the same ideology, which is, theorizing on the patterns of the relative frequency of the linguistic features retrieved and observed. In addition, both modeling ways share the same ultimate purpose of construing the probability profile of a linguistic theory or phenomenon. In general, the corpus-supported approach to SFG is attestable in nature, whose study is based on a large scale of the real linguistic data proof describing and explaining linguistic forms, meanings and functions through attested data and statistical methods. In addition, it belongs to the extended complementary branch of the grand system of SFG. Furthermore, the corpus-supported approach to SFG will refine and advance the development of SFG. The accumulation of evidence from corpus studies produces a more objective and representative account of the nature of language; on the other hand, it has the worth of promoting the theoretical research in CL by providing the foundation for some highly theoretical reasoning.

8.2 Further Research to Be Explored

The interpersonal metafunction, and its evaluation and the thematic cohesive system are not touched upon in this book, because modeling the grammatical senses into some automatically retrievable patterns is much too hard to go on. At present, artificial intelligence technology in processing language is not so advanced that these senses can only be manually annotated. Greater efforts are needed to come closer to and realize the theoretical model of transforming grammatical senses into retrievable forms; meanwhile, some more intelligent linguistic data-processing software tools are to be designed and developed to be competent for marking more abstract meanings with the guidelines discovered in the theoretical modeling. Progress in theoretical modeling and developing more capable software can realize an (semi-)automatic annotation of the interpersonal metafunction and the thematic cohesive system.

Bibliography

Aarts, J. (1999). Towards a new generation of corpus-based English grammars. In *2nd International Conference on Practical Applications in Language Corpora*. Lodz, Poland.

Ädel, A. (2003). *The Use of metadiscourse in argumentative writing by advanced learners and native speakers of English*. PhD dissertation, Göteborg: University of Göteborg.

Aijmer, K. (2008). Introduction. In K. Aijmer & B. Altenberg (Eds.), *Advances in corpus linguistics*. (pp. 1-7). London: Continuum.

Armstrong, E. M. (1991). The potential of cohesion analysis in the analysis and treatment of aphasic discourse. *Clinical Linguistics & Phonetics*, 5(1): 39-51.

Baker, P. (2006). *Using corpora in discourse analysis*. London: Continuum.

Baker, P., Hardie, A., & McEnery, T. (2006). *A glossary of corpus linguistic*. Edinburgh: Edinburgh University Press.

Baldry, A., & Thibault, P. (2006). Multimodal corpus linguistics. In G. Thompson & S. Hunston (Eds.), *System and corpus: Exploring connections*. (pp. 164-183). London: Equinox.

Bateman, J. (1997). *KPML development environment: Multilingual linguistic resource development and sentence generation*. Darmstadt: IPSI.

Bateman, J., & Paris, C. (1991). Constraining the deployment of lexicogrammatical resources during text generation: Towards a computational instantiation of register theory. In E. Ventola (Ed.), *Functional and systemic linguistics: Approaches and uses* (pp. 81-106). Berlin: Mouton de Gruyter.

Biber, D. (2000). *Corpus linguistics*. Beijing: Foreign Language Teaching and

Research Press; Cambridge: Cambridge University Press.

Biber, D., Conrad, S., & Reppen, R. (1998). *Corpus linguistics: Investigating language structure and use.* Cambridge: Cambridge University Press.

Christie, F. (1991). First and second-order registers in education. In E. Ventola (Ed.), *Functional and systemic linguistics: Approaches and uses.* (pp. 77-92). Berlin & New York: Mouton.

Cross, M. (1991). Choice in text: A systemic-functional approach to computer modelling of variant text production. Unpublished PhD dissertation, Sydney: Macquarie University.

Fawcett, R. P., & Tucker, G. H. (1990). Demonstration of GENESYS: A very large semantically based Systemic Functional Grammar. In *Proceedings of the 13th Int. Conf. on Computationalnguistics* (COLING 90).

Fawcett, R. P. (1990). The computer generation of speech with semantically and discoursally motivated intonation. In *Proceedings of Fifth International Workshop on National Language Generation*, 164-173. Pittsburgh.

Firth, J. R. (1957). Modes of meaning. In J. R. Firth (Eds.), *Papers in linguistics 1934—1951.* (pp. 62-87). London & New York: Oxford University Press.

Fries, C. C. (1940). *American English grammar.* New York: Appleton Century.

Fries, C. C. (1957). *The structure of English: An introduction to the construction of English sentences.* London: Longmans, Green.

Goyvaerts, J., & Levithan, S (2009). *Regular expression cookbook.* Sebastopol: O' Reilly Media, Inc.

Gregory, M., & Carroll, S. (1978). *Language and situation: Language varieties in their social context.* London: Routledge and Kegan Paul.

Halliday, M. A. K. (1961). Categories of the theory of grammar. *Word,* 17(3): 242-292.

Halliday, M. A. K. (1962). Linguistics and machine translation. In J. J. Webster (Ed.), *Computational and quantitative studies.* (pp. 20-35). London: Continuum.

Halliday, M. A. K. (1964). Syntax and the consumer. In C. I. J. M. Stuart (Ed.), *Report of the fifteenth annual (first international) round table meeting on linguistics and language* (pp. 11-24). (Reprinted in Halliday and Martin

(1981))Washington, DC: Georgetown University Press.

Halliday, M. A. K. (1966). Some notes on 'deep' grammar. *Journal of Linguistics*, 2(1): 57-67.

Halliday, M. A. K. (1971). Linguistic function and literary style: An enquiry into the language of William Golding's *The Inheritors*. In S. Chatman (Ed), *Literary style: A symposium*. New York: Oxford University Press.

Halliday, M. A. K. (1973). *Explorations in the functions of language*. London: Edward Arnold.

Halliday, M. A. K. (1976). System and function in language. In G. R. Kress (Ed.), *Halliday: System and function in language: Selected papers*. (pp. 238-244). London: Oxford University Press.

Halliday, M. A. K. (1977). "Ideas about Language". *Occasional Papers* 1. Applied Linguistics Association of Australia. pp. 32-55.

Halliday, M. A. K. (1978). *Language as social semiotic: The social interpretation of language and meaning*. London: Edward Arnold.

Halliday, M. A. K. (1982). How is a text like a clause?. In S. Allen (Ed.) *Text processing: Text analysis and generation, text typology and attribution. (Proceedings of Nobel symposium 51)*. (pp. 209-224). Stockholm: Almgvist & Wiksell International.

Halliday, M. A. K. (1985). *An introduction to functional grammar*. London: Edward Arnold.

Halliday, M. A. K. (1987). Language and the order of nature. In N. Fabb, et al. (Eds.) *The linguistics of writing: Arguments between language and literature*. (pp. 135-154). Manchester: Manchester University Press.

Halliday, M. A. K. (1988). On the language of physical science. In M. Ghadessy (Ed.), *Registers of written English: Situational factors and linguistic features*. New York: Pinter Publishers.

Halliday, M. A. K. (1991a). Towards probabilistic interpretations. In J. J. Webster (Ed.), *Computational and quantitative studies*. (pp. 42-62). London: Continuum.

Halliday, M. A. K. (1991b). Corpus studies and probabilistic grammar. In J. J. Webster (Ed.), *Computational and quantitative studies*. (pp. 63-75). London:

Continuum.

Halliday, M. A. K. (1991c). Corpus studies and probabilistic grammar. In K. Ajjmeretal & B. Altenberg. (Eds.). *English corpus linguistics*. London: Longman.

Halliday, M. A. K. (1992). Language as system and language as instance: The corpus as a theoretical construct. In J. J. Webster (Ed.), *Computational and quantitative studies*. (pp. 76-92). London: Continuum.

Halliday, M. A. K. (1993a). Quantitative studies and probabilities in grammar. In J. Webster (Ed.). *Computational and quantitative studies* (Vol. 6 in the collected works of M. A. K. Halliday). (pp.130-156). Beijing: Peking University Press.

Halliday, M. A. K. (1993b). A quantitative study of polarity and primary tense in the English finite clause. In J. J. Webster (Ed.), *Computational and quantitative studies*. (pp. 93-129). London: Continuum.

Halliday, M. A. K. (1993c). Language as system and language as instance: The corpus as a theoretical construct. In M. Hoey (Ed.), *Data, description, discourse*. London: Harper Collins Publisher.

Halliday, M. A. K. (1994). So you say 'pass'... thank you three muchly. In A. D. Grimshaw (Ed.), *What's going on here: Complementary studies of professional talk* (pp. 175-229). Norwood, NJ: Ablex.

Halliday, M. A. K. (1996). On grammar and grammatics. In R. Hasan, C. Cloran & D. Butt (Eds.), *Functional descriptions: Theory into practice*. (pp. 1-38). Amsterdam: Benjamins.

Halliday, M. A. K. (2002a). The spoken language corpus: A foundation for grammatical theory. In J. J. Webster (Ed.), *Computational and quantitative studies*. (pp. 153-189). London: Continuum.

Halliday, M. A. K. (2002b). Computing meanings: Some reflections on past experience and present prospects. In G. W. Huang (Ed.), *Discourse and language functions*. (pp. 3-25). Beijing: Foreign Language Teaching and Research Press.

Halliday, M. A. K. (2002c). *Linguistic studies of text and discourse*. London: Continuum.

Halliday, M. A. K. (2004a). *An introduction to functional grammar* (3rd ed.). London: Arnold.

Halliday, M. A. K. (2004b). Lexicology. In M. A. K Halliday et al. (Eds.), *Lexicology and corpus linguistics.* (pp. 1-22). London: Continuum.

Halliday, M. A. K. (2005). Computational and quantitative studies. In J. Webster (Ed.), *The collected works of M. A. K. Halliday, Vol. 6.* London and New York: Continuum.

Halliday, M. A. K. (2006). *Linguistic studies of text and discourse* (collected works of M. A. K. Halliday). London and New York: Continuum.

Halliday, M. A. K. (2008). *An introduction to functional grammar* (3rd ed.). Beijing: Foreign Language Teaching and Research Press.

Halliday, M. A. K. et al. *An introduction to functional grammar.* London: Hodder Arnold.

Halliday, M. A. K., & Hasan, R. (1976). *Cohesion in English.* London: Longman.

Halliday, M. A. K., & Hasan, R. (1985). *Language, context and text: A social semiotic perspective.* Geelong: Deakin University Press.

Halliday, M. A. K., & Hasan, R. (1994). *Bahasa, konteks, dan teks: aspek aspek bahasa dala pandangan semiotika sosial.* (Terjemahar Assruddin B.Tou). Yogyakarya: Gadjah Mada University Press. (The original was published in 1985 by Deakin University, Victoria).

Halliday, M. A. K., & Martin, J. R. (Ed.). (1981). *Readings in systemic linguistics.* London: Batsford.

Halliday, M. A. K., & Matthiessen, C. M. I. M. (1999). *Construing experience: A language-based approach to cognition.* London: Cassell.

Halliday, M. A. K., Teubert, W., Yallop, C., & Cermakova, A. (2004). *Lexicology and corpus linguistics.* London and New York: Continuum.

Halliday, M. A. K., 胡壮麟 (Hu, Z. L.), & 朱永生 (Zhu, Y. S.). (2010). Interviewing Professor M. A. K. Halliday by Hu Zhuanglin and Zhu Yongsheng. 中国外语, 7(6): 17-24.

Hasan, R. (1987). The grammarian's dream: Lexis as most delicate grammar. In M. A. K. Halliday & R. Fawcett (Eds.), *New developments in systemic linguistics.* (pp. 184-211). London: Pinter.

Hoey, M. (2003). What's in a word?. *English Teaching Professional*, 82(4): 91-94.

Hoey, M. (2004). Textual colligation: A special kind of lexical priming. *Language & Computers*, 49(1): 171-194.

Hoey, M. (2005). *Lexical priming: A new theory of words and language*. London: Routledge.

Hoey, M. (2006). Language as a choice: What is chosen?. In G. Thompson & S. Hunston (Eds.), *System and corpus: Exploring connections*. (pp. 37-54). London: Equinox.

Hori, M. (2006). Pain expression in Japanese. In G. Thompson & S. Hunston (Eds.), *System and corpus: Exploring connections*. (pp. 206-225). London: Equinox.

Hunston, S. (2002). *Corpora in applied linguistics*. Cambridge: Cambridge University Press.

Hunston, S. (2006). Phraseology and system: A contribution to the debate?. In G. Thompson & S. Hunston (Eds.), *System and corpus: Exploring connections*. (pp. 55-80). London: Equinox.

Hunston, S., & Francis G. (2000). *Pattern grammar: A corpus-driven approach to the lexical grammar of English*. Amsterdam & Philadelphia: Benjamins.

Hyland, K. (2004). Disciplinary interactions: Metadiscourse in L2 postgraduate writing. *Journal of Second Language Writing*, 13 (2): 133-151.

Kaltenbacher, M. (2006). Culture related linguistic differences in tourist websites: The emotive and the factual: A corpus analysis within the framework of Appraisal. In G. Thompson & S. Hunston (Eds.), *System and corpus: Exploring connections*. (pp. 269-292). London and Oakville: Equinox Publishing Ltd.

Kasper, R. (1988). Systemic grammar and functional unification grammar. In J. Benson &W. Greaves (Eds.), *Systemic functional approaches to discourse*. (pp. 58-74). Norwood, NJ: Ablex.

Kawaguchi Y. (2007). Introduction. In Y. Kawaguchi (Ed.), *Corpus-based perspectives in linguistics*. (pp. 31-38). Amsterdam: Benjamins.

Kennedy, G. (1998). *An introduction to corpus linguistics*. London: Longman.

Leech, G. (1965). "This bread I break": Language and interpretation. *Review of English Literature*, 6(2): 66-75.

Leech, G. (1992). Corpora and theories of linguistic performance. In J. Svartvik (Ed.), *Directions in corpus linguistics*. (pp. 105-122). Berlin: Mouton de Gruyter.

Louw, B. (1993). Irony in the text or insincerity in the writer?. In M. Baker, G. Francis & E. Tognini-Bonelli (Eds.), *Text and technology: In honour of John Sinclair*. (pp. 151-163). Amsterdam: John Benjamins.

Mahlberg, M. (2006). Lexical cohesion: Corpus linguistic theory and its application in ELT. *Special Issue of the International Journal of Corpus Linguistics*, 11(3): 363-383.

Mair, C. (2009). Corpus linguistics meets sociolinguistics: The role of corpus evidence in the study of sociolinguistic variation and change. In A. Renouf & A. Kehoe (Eds.), *Corpus Lnguistics: Refinements and Reassessments*. (pp. 7-32). Amsterdam: Rodopi.

Mann W., & Matthiessen C. M. I. M. (1983). Nigel: A systemic grammar for text generation. In *Systemic perspectives on discourse selected papers from international systemics workshop*. (pp.79-81). London: Ablex Publishers Company.

Martin, J. R. (1992). *English text: System and structure*. Amsterdam: John Benjamins.

Matthiessen, C. M. I. M. (1988) Representational issues in systemic functional grammar. In J. D. Benson & W. S. Greaves (Eds), *Systemic perspectives on discourse: Selected papers from the 9th international systemic workshop* (Vol. 1). (pp. 136-175). Norwood, NJ: Ablex.

Matthiessen, C. M. I. M. (1993). Register in the round: Diversity in a unified theory of register analysis. In M. Ghadessy (Eds.), *Register analysis: Theory and practice*. (pp. 221-292). London: Pinter.

Matthiessen, C. M. I. M. (1995). *Lexicogrammatical cartography: English systems*. Tokyo: International Language Sciences Publishers.

Matthiessen, C. M. I. M. (2002). Lexicogrammar in discourse development: Logogenetic patterns of wording. In G. Huang & Z. Wang (Eds.), *Discourse and language functions*. (pp. 91-127). Shanghai: Foreign Language Teaching and Research Press.

Matthiessen, C. M. I. M. (2006). Frequency profiles of some basic grammatical system: An interim report. In G. Thompson & S. Hunston (Eds.). *System and corpus: Exploring connections*. (pp. 81-142). London: Equinox.

Matthiessen, C. M. I. M. (2010). Systemic functional linguistics developing. *Annual Review of Functional Linguistics*, 2: 8-63.

Matthiessen, C. M. I. M., & Bateman, J. A. (1991). *Systemic linguistics and text generation: Experiences from Japanese and English*. London: Pinter.

Matthiessen, C. M. I. M. et al. (1998). The Multex generator and its environment: Application and development. Proceedings of the International Generation Workshop '98, August '98, Niagara-on-the-Lake. 228-237.

Matthiessen, C. M. I. M., & Nesbitt, C. (1996). On the idea of theory-neutral descriptions. In R. Hasan, C. Cloran & D. Butt (Eds.), *Functional descriptions: Theory in practice*. (pp.39-85). Amsterdam: Benjamins.

Matthiessen, C. M. I. M., O'Donnell, M., & Zeng, L. (1991). Discourse Analysis and the Need for Functionally Complex Grammars in Parsing. In *Proceedings of the 2nd Japan-Australia Symposium on Natural Language Processing*, Japan.

McEnery, T., & Andrew, W. (2001). *Corpus linguistics: An introduction* (2nd ed.). Edinburgh: Edinburgh University Press.

McEnery T., & Wilson A. (1996). *Corpus linguistics*. Edinburgh: Edinburgh University Press.

Neal, A. (2002). More delicate Transitivity: Extending the PROCESS TYPE system networks for English to include full semantic classifications. Doctoral dissertation, Cardiff: Cardiff University.

Nesbitt, C. (1994). Construing linguistic resources: Consumer perspectives. Unpublished doctoral dissertation, Department of Linguistics, Sydney: University of Sydney.

Nesbitt, C., & Plum, G. (1988). Probabilities in a systemic grammar: The clause complex in English. In R. P. Fawcett & D. J. Young (Eds.), *New developments in systemic linguistics 2: Theory and application*. (pp. 6-38). London & New

York: Pinter.

Nesi, H., & Basturkmen, H. (2009). Lexical bundles and discourse signalling in academic lectures. In J. Flowerdew & M. Mahlberg (Eds.), *Lexical cohesion and corpus linguistics.* (pp. 23-44). Amsterdam: Benjamins.

O'Donnell, M. (1994). From theory to implementations: Analysis and generation with systemic grammar. Doctoral dissertation, Sydney: University of Sydney.

O'Donnell, M. (2002). Automating the coding of semantic patterns: Applying machine learning to corpus linguistics. Paper presented at the meeting of 29th International Systemic Functional Congress, Liverpool.

Palmer, H. E., & Hornby, A. S. (1933). *Second interim report on English collocations.* Tokyo: Institute for research in English Teaching.

Partington, A. (1998). *Patterns and meanings: Using corpora for English language research and teaching.* Amsterdam: Benjamins.

Renouf, A. (2005). Corpus linguistics: Past and present // 卫乃兴，等，语料库应用研究．上海：上海外语教育出版社．

Rothery, J. (1989). Learning about language. In R. Hasan & J. Martin (Eds.). *Learning language, learning culture.* (pp. 67-94). Norwood, NJ: Ablex.

Sampson, G. R. (1987). Probabilistic models of analysis. In R. G. Garside et al. (Eds.), *The computational analysis of English: A corpus-based approach.* London: Longman.

Sharoff, S. (2006). How to handle lexical semantics in SFL: A corpus study of purposes for using size adjectives. In G. Thompson & S. Hunston (Eds.), *System and corpus: Exploring connections.* (pp. 184-205). London: Equinox.

Sinclair, J. (1991). *Corpus concordance collocation.* Oxford: Oxford University Press.

Sinclair, J. (2003). *Reading concordance.* London: Routledge.

Sinclair, J. (2004). *Trust the text.* London: Routledge.

Stubblebine, T. (2007). *Regular expression pocket reference* (2nd ed.). Sebastopol: O' Reilly Media, Inc.

Stubbs, M. (1996). *Text and corpus analysis.* Oxford: Blackwell.

Stubbs, M. (2001). Words and phrases: Corpus studies of lexical semantics. *Nature,* 71(4): 90-92.

Stubbs, M. (2006). Corpus analysis: The state of the art and three types of unanswered questions. In G. Thompson & S. Hunston (Eds.), *System and corpus: Exploring connections*. (pp. 15-36). London: Equinox.

Teich, E. (1999). System-oriented and text-oriented Comparative linguistic research: Cross-linguistic variation in translation. *Languages in Contrast*, 2(2): 187-210.

Teubert, W. (2004). Language and corpus linguistics. In M. A. K. Halliday et al. (Eds.), *Lexicology and corpus linguistics*. (pp. 73-112). London & New York: Continuum.

Teubert, W. (2007). *Corpus linguistics: A short introduction*. London: Continuum.

Teubert, W., & A. Čermáková. (2004). Directions in Corpus Linguistics. In M. A. K. Halliday. et al. (Eds.), *Lexicology and corpus linguistics*. (pp. 113-65). London & New York: Continuum.

Thompson, G. (2006). System and corpus: Two traditions with a common ground. In G. Thompson & S. Hunston (Eds.), *System and corpus: Exploring connections*. (pp. 1-14). London: Equinox

Tognini-Bonelli, E. (2001). *Corpus linguistics at work*. Amsterdam: Benjamins.

Tucker, G. (2006). Systemic incorporation: On the relationship between corpus and systemic functional grammar. In G. Thompson & S. Hunston (Eds.), *System and corpus: Exploring connections*. (pp. 81-102). London: Equinox.

Webster, J. J. (Ed.). (2002). *Computational and quantitative studies*. London: Continuum.

Webster, J. J. (Ed.). (2005). *The collected works of M.A. K. Halliday, Vol. 6*. London and New York: Continuum.

Wu, C. Z. (2000). *Modelling linguistic resources*. Doctoral dissertation, Sydney: Macquarie University.

Wu, C. Z. (2006). Exploring English nominal groups modified by embedded clauses in translation: A corpus-based approach. In The International Conference on Translation and Interdisciplinary Studies, Shanghai.

Yallop, C. (2004). Words and meaning. In M. A. K. Halliday et al. (Eds.), *Lexicology and corpus linguistics*. (pp. 23-70). London: Continuum.

Zeng, L. (1996). Planning text in an integrated multilingual meaning space. PhD dissertation. Sydney: University of Sydney.

桂诗春 (Gui, S.-C.) (2004). 以概率为基础的语言研究. 外语教学与研究, 36(1): 3-9.

何安平 (He, A.-P) (1998). 英语会话中的简短反馈语. 现代汉语, (1): 75, 74, 76-82.

何安平 (He, A.-P.) (2004). 语料库语言学与英语教学. 北京: 外语教学与研究出版社.

李文中 (Li, W.-Z.) (2010). 语料库语言学的研究视野. 解放军外国语学院学报, 33(2): 37-40, 72, 127.

潘宗乾 (Pan, Z.-Q.) (2003). 英汉双解英语同义词词典. 北京: 外语教学与研究出版社.

濮建忠 (Pu, J.-Z.) (2010). 语料库与语言一元化研究. 解放军外国语学院学报, 33(2): 41-44, 127.

卫乃兴 (Wei, N.-X.) (2007). John Sinclair的语言学遗产——其思想与方法评述. 外国语, 170(3): 14-19.

卫乃兴 (Wei, N.-X.) (2009). 语料库语言学的方法论及相关理念. 外语研究, 117(5): 36-42.

卫乃兴, 李文中, 濮建忠 (Wei, N.-X., Li, W. -Z., & Pu, J. -Z.) (2005). 语料库应用研究. 上海: 上海外语教育出版社.

杨惠中 (Yang, H.-Z.) (2002). 语料库语言学导论. 上海: 上海外语教育出版社.

张凤芝, 严亚莉, 干红梅 (Zhang, F.-Z., Yan, Y.-L. & Gan, H.-M.) (2002). 语言学科建设高级专家座谈会综述. 暨南大学华文学院学报, 20(4): 76-79.

宗成庆 (Zong, C.-Q.) (2008). 统计自然语言处理. 北京: 清华大学出版社.

Index

A

anaphora   142

anaphoric reference   142, 152

AntConc   128, 157

antonymy   125, 126, 127, 132

API

B

British National Corpus (BNC)   105

Brown Corpus   71

C

Cardiff grammar   38, 43

cataphoric reference   142, 152

CLAWS   103, 104, 114, 120

Codes for the Human Analysis of Transcripts   70

cohesion   12, 122, 123, 124, 125, 132

colligation   18, 75

Collins COBUILD English Dictionary   24

collocation   23, 50, 55, 57, 61, 71, 126

competence   31

computational linguistics   16, 33